# The Beginner's Guide to

# Mind, Body & Spirit

# The Beginner's Guide to
# Mind, Body & Spirit

## Rosalind Widdowson

### NEW LINE BOOKS

# CONTENTS

# CONTENTS

# CONTENTS

# AROMATHERAPY

## INTRODUCTION

*My interest in natural therapies started in my early childhood. I lived in Africa and was surrounded by tropical fruit and plants. Our garden was a haven for any naturalist and I loved nothing better than to wander through the avenues of lemons, peaches and apricot trees when laden with blossom. Their heavenly scent transported my senses and gave me a feeling of healthy well-being.*

*In my naivety, and perhaps as a foretaste of things to come, I spent much of my free time mixing and boiling various plants, adding petals to water in glass bottles and jars, in an effort to capture these divine properties. I imagined them to be a potent elixir which would promote good health and prolong life. Even my dolls were treated with rejuvenating mud packs! It was quite natural through my adult years that I should develop a professional interest in diet, aromatherapy and massage. Through study and experimentation with various forms of diet and nutrition I have explored the numerous ways in which natural products can promote health and beauty.*

*My students and I like nothing better than to make up our own treatments, utilizing herbs and plants from the garden. Our experiments range from compresses, body and face scrubs made from groundnuts, citrus peel, oats and essential oils, to face masks of avocado or tropical fruits which revitalize the skin and give the face a new lustre.*

*I am always delighted to hear of positive results from my students like Jan B. who recently started to treat her twin boys' psoriasis by encouraging them to soak in an aromatherapy bath for 20 minutes, every other night. She blends together two drops of geranium oil to 5ml of dispersing bath oil and adds five drops of this blended mix to their bath. In a few short weeks the results have been dramatic and their skin is nearly clear.*

*Scented oils can be used in your home in all sorts of inventive ways … by spraying over freshly laundered bed linen, silk or fresh herb and flower arrangements. Sensual oils such as ylang ylang are an ideal prelude to the best kind of pillow talk.*

*Aromatherapy is increasingly finding acceptance as a complementary treatment that can go hand in hand with conventional medicine. I hope you enjoy reading and using my book and that you will be encouraged to further your study of the many natural ways that plants and trees can heal and enhance your life.*

*My aim in using an 'Easy Steps' technique is to encourage you in a practical interest that will be of help to you, your family and friends. The one technique which I feel is an essential prelude to any treatment is a physical and mental cleansing of negative energies. All treatments need to be given in a relaxed, loving and compassionate manner but remember, all natural healing energy flows through us from the Universal Source rather than from us as individuals. You should not end up feeling drained but be uplifted and relaxed by the whole experience. It is important to connect physically with the earth every day and the careful nurture of your own plants and garden will enhance your practice of aromatherapy. Cultivating a deep appreciation of nature's healing energies will, in itself, help you develop more and varied ways of using your own natural healing energies in everyday life.*

*I wish you a wealth of health and happiness.*

*Rosalind*

Aromatherapy has a fascinating history. Its earliest recorded use is in China as long ago as 4,000 B.C. The techniques of pressing, steeping, boiling and drying were used to obtain aromatic essences and oils from flowers, leaves, woods, gums and resins. The Chinese were probably among the first people to use plant oils for medicinal purposes.

The Egyptians, Persians and Babylonians were known to have a passion for beautiful perfumes and made scented waters from a distillation of rose petals and orange blossoms. They used lavish amounts of perfumed oils and lotions in baths and cosmetics as an aid to personal grooming. The Egyptian pharaohs were ritually embalmed with specific ingredients believed to delay decomposition, while the living made use of similar medicinal substances for their own healing purposes. It was the Persian philosopher and physician, Avicenna, who was among the first to refine the distillation process whereby much purer essential oils were produced.

Due to the increasing demand for these precious ingredients, trade routes were established with the Greeks and Romans who had extensive contacts, offering an expanded range of ingredients from all over the known world. It was the Romans, in turn, who brought the idea to Britain.

There are records of the use of plant oils in Europe from the 13th

century but it was not until the 17th century that their uses were codified by Nicholas Culpeper. He was to write the first herbal/medicinal handbook describing remedies derived from hundreds of plants. His research revealed just how essential oils work: by penetrating the skin via the extra-cellular liquids to reach the circulatory and lymphatic systems they are, in turn, carried to the inner organs. This basic process varies enormously in each individual, sometimes taking as little as half and hour and in others up to 12 hours to complete the process. Skin penetration takes only a few minutes.

The advent of chemical substitutes in the 19th century almost destroyed the demand for natural oils although they did not have the same medicinal properties or efficacy. True essential oils contain a complex mixture of alcohols, esters, hydrocarbons, aldehydes, ketones, phenols, terpene alcohol and acids. Although most of the elements are known today, chemists are still unable to reconstitute an essential oil with total accuracy.

It was a French chemist, René Gattefosse, who pioneered the use of plant oils in modern medicine after healing his own burns with lavender oil. He went on to successfully treat many severe cases of burns in the First World War and developed the wide range of healing oils with which we are familiar today. From the 1940s onwards, Marguérite Maury, the

Austrian biochemist and beautician, experimented with the holistic use of essential oils, i.e. prescribing treatments for individuals while taking account of various imbalances of mind, body and emotions. Her extensive research is responsible for developing aromatherapy massage and various beauty and skin care treatments as we know them today. She was the first person to establish the technique of applying essential oils diluted in pure vegetable oils (base/carrier) for massage.

Over the past 25 years there has been an upsurge of interest in the numerous therapeutic uses of essential oils. There exists a deep desire to preserve some of nature's treasured gifts in an age where there is widespread revulsion against the destructive elements of materialism on our environment. Nature is being recognized anew as a treasure-trove of valuable gifts which can heal both humankind as well as the environment.

## HOW ESSENTIAL OILS ARE PRODUCED

Essential oils are obtained from various parts of plants and trees. Just about every constituent part can be used, at some time or another. Roots, stalks, barks, leaves, flowers and blossoms, seeds, nuts, fruits and resins – all have yielded valuable ingredients to the aromatherapist's art. As we know, each oil is made up of numerous organic molecules and are extremely complex substances. Some oils have up to 250 different constituents which is why it is almost impossible to successfully reproduce them by synthetic means. They are extracted from vegetable matter by the following processes:

**1  Maceration** (softening by steeping). Used for thousands of years, this is perhaps the oldest method of producing an 'infused oil'. Though it does not, strictly speaking, produce an essential oil, which is extracted directly from the plant, this process will nonetheless produce a substance which has absorbed many of the plant's therapeutic properties and can be used in broadly the same manner as its corresponding essential oil.

To commercially produce a perfumed essence or 'floral oil' of the highest quality,  flowers such as jasmine, rose and orange blossom are spread on trays which contain a bland vegetable oil. The process by which oil

becomes saturated with perfume is called 'enfleurage' and it is only after months of continuous replenishment that the process of 'defleurage' can be applied using a solvent to separate out the aromatic substances. This long and painstaking process is, of course, reflected in the cost of the final product.

You can easily and cheaply repeat this process for yourself. Take a large clean jar and fill it one third full with your chosen petals or leaves (experiment with apple, orange, peach or cherry blossom, jasmine, honeysuckle etc.) Fill the jar almost to the top with a good quality bland vegetable oil (almond, grape-seed, sesame, sunflower). Cover the top, excluding as much air as possible, and store in a warm place such as an airing cupboard, or above a central heating boiler or Aga. When the petals turn brown remove and replace with a fresh batch. Do this three or four times until you obtain the strength of perfume you require. Lastly, put through a fine strainer to remove any debris which may remain.

**2    Distillation.** This is the main method by which essential oils are obtained from plants The process

involves filling large vats with plant material which is steamed at high pressure. The steam and essential oil vapour is then cooled, condensed and collected.

**3 Expression.** Citrus oils are obtained in this way by simply expressing (squeezing) the peel of the fruit which contains the essential oil droplets. Lemon, lime, mandarin, orange, tangerine and bergamot oils are all obtained in this way.

## THE DIFFERENCE BETWEEN AN ESSENTIAL OIL AND AN ESSENCE

You must use genuine essential oils – the pure natural oil is more active than synthetically-produced oils and less likely to cause adverse reactions. The whole aromatic essence is more powerful than its components, for example, the essential oil of Eucalyptus is more powerful than its derivative Eucalyptol. Chemically, essential oils are made up of a large number of elements including alcohols, esters, hydrocarbons, aldehydes, ketones, phenols, terpene alcohol and acids. Most of the elements are known but others have yet to be discovered and chemists are unable to reconstitute an essential oil with total accuracy.

You may find oils or products marked 'essence'. These are chemically-synthesized and are usually cheaper although, curiously enough, this is not always the case. You should only pur-

chase products marked 'pure essential oil' and always check the origin of the brand.

## HOW CARRIER OILS ARE USED

Essential Oils are extremely powerful concentrated agents and are sometimes quite toxic in their pure state. Except in very rare cases they are not used directly on the skin. Carrier oils, or base oils must therefore be used to dilute them to safe proportions and provide the lubrication necessary to allow the masseur's hands to glide, without friction, over the skin. In addition, this largely neutral vegetable medium is readily absorbed through the pores of the skin during massage. It is by this action that the essential oil passes into the bloodstream and travels to the body's vital organs, thus achieving the desired therapeutic effect. The range includes sunflower, safflower, soya, sesame, grape-seed, sweet almond, olive, avocado, coconut, wheatgerm, corn, hazelnut, jojoba and, my personal favourites, peach and apricot kernel. Although each would have a complementary healing property of its own, the most popular are the lighter and unperfumed oils such as sunflower, safflower, grape-seed, sesame and sweet almond. With practice and experience you may wish to experiment with combinations of carrier oils for different effects. The best quality oils are cold-pressed and 'vir-

gin', preferably a combination of both, untreated by heat and free from chemical additives.

## BLENDING ESSENTIAL AND CARRIER OILS

In general terms you would expect to dilute your chosen essential oil(s) in a 3 per cent solution with your carrier oil. This amounts to 3 drops of essential oil(s) to 5ml of carrier oil. Either use a glass dispensing jug purchased from a chemist or a 5ml medicine-spoon. To estimate quantities suitable for your particular partner, see section on 'Buying, Storing and Preparing Oils' on pages 26/28.

> **IMPORTANT NOTE**
> It must be remembered that a blend of essential oils and its carrier oil is primarily a 'treatment'. The method of application, i.e. massage, is strictly the secondary consideration. Dosage can be quite crucial when dealing with a number of medical conditions or when your partner is in a vulnerable, sensitive, or distressed mood. Please observe the following guidelines as closely as possible.

## BASIL

*Uplifting, refreshing, mind-clearing, invigorating, stimulating, powerfully antiseptic, tonic, aphrodisiac, antispasmodic.*

**Aroma:** Refreshing, rather like camphor.

**Therapeutic Benefits:** Excellent nerve tonic, eases indigestion, digestive problems (LM abdomen); tired overworked muscles; traditional remedy for respiratory infections such as bronchitis, whooping cough, fever (CBM, SI); helps reduce engorged breasts (CC); improves circulation; good for skin tone; relieves headaches, migraine colds (LM); regulates menstrual cycle, helps with scanty and painful periods (LM-lower abdomen); improves concentration, clarifies the mind, lifts mental fatigue, anxiety and depression.

**Other Uses:** In insect repellents. Cooking.

**Caution:** Best avoided during pregnancy. In excess can cause grogginess and depression.

## BAY

*Uplifting, antiseptic, tonic, analgesic.*

**Aroma:** Warm, pungent, spicy.

**Therapeutic Benefits:** Relieves bronchitis, colds, flu, sinusitis (SI); improves digestion; soothes rheumatism (B, LM). A good general tonic, helps with insomnia.

**Other Uses:** Chew as a breath freshener, use in hair care, cooking, perfumes.

## BENZOIN

*Penetrating, warming, soothing, stimulating, energizing.*

**Aroma:** Vanilla-like scent.

**Therapeutic Benefits:** Relieves coughs, colds, flu, laryngitis and sore throats (SL); stimulates circulation, expels gas, increases flow of urine. Heals skin lesions, cracked and chapped hands, chilblains (SL, CR); soothes and alleviates loneliness, depression, anxiety (CBM).

**Other Uses:** In incense to ward off 'evil spirits'. Included in traditional cough medicines (Friar's Balsam).

**Caution:** Excessive amounts can cause drowsiness.

## BERGAMOT

*Powerfully uplifting, excellent anti-depressant, nerve sedative, strongly antiseptic, regulating, cooling, deodorizing, anti-viral.*

**Aroma:** Delightful citrus scent.

**Therapeutic Benefits:** Eases cystitis, urethritis, (B, D – but diluted to half or one per cent in boiled and cooled water); an antiseptic used in skin care for acne, oiliness, infections, ulcers, wounds (GD, NA), cold sores, shingles (neat or diluted in alcohol); lung conditions, bronchitis (SI); loss of appetite and anorexia nervosa; very best oil for depression and anxiety – uplifts mood (CBM, B, VP personal perfume).

**Other Uses:** Flavours Earl Grey tea, useful as an insect repellent, effective

17

deodorant, fragrant room freshener.
**Caution:** Never use undiluted, do not sunbathe after use. Can cause skin pigmentation with increased risk of skin cancer.

## BLACK PEPPER

*Stimulating, warming, invigorating, antispasmodic, tonic.*
**Aroma:** Pungent and spicy.
**Therapeutic Benefits:** Relieves fever (used in small amounts); stimulates circulation; detoxifies by helping remove phlegm; strengthens muscles and eases aches, pains, fatigue; aids digestion, stimulates appetite, invigorates a sluggish digestive system (LM abdomen).
**Other Uses:** Cooking. A little black pepper adds 'lift' to any blend of oil(s).
**Caution:** Use in small quantities or low proportions in a blend or it may cause skin irritation.

## CAMOMILE

*Soothing/sedative, calming, best anti-inflammatory, best anti-allergenic, analgesic/pain relieving, disinfectant, a gentle anti-depressant.*
**Aroma:** Distinctive apple-like scent.
**Therapeutic Benefits**: Eases indigestion, aids digestion and reduces internal inflammatory conditions – particularly digestive – such as colitis, gastritis and diarrhoea (T, LM-abdomen, HC); soothes ulcers (T), sprains, swollen and

painful joints, bursitis (housemaid's knee)(CC), allergies – whether physically or emotionally induced (B,T), otitis (ear infection)(LM, HC), menstrual problems (periods), menopause; combats fluid retention, premenstrual tension, (B, CBM, T); cystitis and urinary infections (T,HC), aches and pains in both muscles and organs (IM), rheumatism, arthritis (LM, B, T, SL, CR), boils, abscesses, infected cuts, splinters (HC), soothes dermatitis, eczema, burns, sores, rashes, psoriasis, herpes (SL, CR, B); calms nerves, eases depression, irritability, insomnia, anxiety (CBM, T), epilepsy – most effective in controlling seizures (CBM, perfume).
**Other Uses:** Shampoo for highlighting and conditioning blond hair.
**Caution:** Although low in toxicity, it is wise to use in low dosages on children. Should not be used in early months of pregnancy.

## CEDARWOOD

*Stabilizing, regulating, powerfully antiseptic, mildly astringent, tonic, stimulating, aphrodisiac.*
**Aroma:** Mild woody scent.
**Therapeutic Benefits:** Aids respiratory system by breaking down mucus and relieves catarrh, bronchitis. Diuretic, useful in cystitis and urinary tract infections. Relieves arthritis, rheumatism. Good for skin complaints, acne, alopecia, dandruff,

eczema. Reduces stress and tension. (CBM, NI).
**Other Uses:** As an insect and moth repellent. Can be used as incense and in aftershave and male perfumes.
**Caution:** Do not use during pregnancy. High doses may cause skin irritation.

## CINNAMON

*Warming, uplifting, stimulating, strongly antiseptic, antispasmodic, aphrodisiac.*
**Aroma:** Warm, spicy and peppery.
**Therapeutic Benefits:** Warming oil especially good for exhaustion caused by colds and coughs, flu. Stimulating tonic for the heart and circulation; improves digestion, soothes stomach ache and nausea, diarrhoea, muscular pain (HC, LM), fatigue and depression (CBM, HC, NI).
**Other Uses:** In incense, pot-pourri, cooking.
**Caution:** Use only in very low dosages.

## CLARY SAGE

*Both a euphoric and powerful relaxant. It is warming, an antispasmodic, good tonic and an aphrodisiac.*
**Aroma:** Nutty, spicy fragrance.
**Therapeutic Benefits:** Relieves stress, anxiety, tension, prolonged mental or emotional stress, insomnia, asthma, migraine, digestive problems, cramps and colicky pains, (LM-abdomen, HC), menstrual cramps; regulates

scanty or missed periods, post-natal debilitation; combats night sweats, menopausal problems.
**Other Uses:** Shampoo.
**Caution:** Do not take alcohol after treatment as it can lead to extreme drunkeness and vivid nightmares. Can induce drowsiness, so do nor drive or operate machinery after a treatment. Avoid during pregnancy.

### EUCALYPTUS
*Stimulating, strongly antiseptic, a powerful bactericide, anti-viral, anti-inflammatory, an effective diuretic.*
**Aroma:** Penetrating camphorous smell.
**Therapeutic Benefits:** The famed decongesting inhalation so excellent for respiratory infections and inflammations such as fever (lowers temperature), coughs, colds, flu, tuberculosis, bronchitis, catarrh, sinusitis, pneumonia, asthma (LM-chest, SI, B, VP). Combats urinary tract infections and cystitis. Relieves rheumatism, muscular pains, fibrositis, migraines. Useful for skin infections, cold sores, shingles, (NA, NI, B)
**Other Uses:** Used widely in cough and cold medicines and inhalants. Effective insect repellent.
**Caution:** Large dosages can irritate the skin.

### FENNEL
*Stimulating, detoxifying, diuretic.*
**Aroma:** Aniseed-like smell.
**Therapeutic Benefits:** Excellent

digestive remedy, kidney stones; relieves nausea, flatulence, obesity, hiccups, indigestion, colitis, cellulite; decreases appetite, useful for urinary tract infections, menopausal problems, nausea, cellulitis (T); counter-balances alcohol poisoning;

increases milk yield during pregnancy.
**Other Uses:** Flavouring for toothpaste, medicines (flatulence and indigestion), gripe water.
**Caution:** Not to be used on young children or by epileptics.

## FRANKINCENSE

*Uplifting, rejuvenating, relaxing, tonic.*

**Aroma:** Fresh, spicy and somewhat camphorous.

**Therapeutic Benefits:** Aids concentration and meditation, slows and deepens breathing, comforting for states of anxiety and asthma attacks; expectorant for respiratory infections (VP, SI) such as bronchitis with catarrh, coughs, colds, laryngitis; rejuvenates ageing skin (CBM, B); helps urinary tract infections (B, LM).

**Other Uses:** In incense as an aid to meditation.

## GERANIUM

*Balancing, uplifting, deodorizing, diuretic, astringent, an anti-depressant, antiseptic, anti-inflammatory and antibacterial.*

**Aroma:** Floral, sweet and refreshing.

**Therapeutic Benefits:** Skin care (all types), balances production of sebum, relieves chilblains (B), wounds – stops bleeding; hormone balancer, relieves premenstrual tension, menopausal problems; helps urinary tract infections, fluid retention, cellulitis, oedema, nervous tension, depression (CBM).

**Other Uses:** As an insect repellent, cosmetic and perfume ingredient.

## HYSSOP

*Stimulating, sedative, disinfectant, tonic.*

**Aroma:** Spicy and aromatic.

**Therapeutic Benefits:** Powerful effect on respiratory tract and chest infections, bronchitis, catarrh, coughs, colds (LM-chest, neck, head, SI, VP); skin disorders, cuts and bruises (CR, HC).

**Other Uses:** Perfumes, liqueurs (Chartreuse), cough mixtures.

**Caution:** Rather toxic – use only in very small doses. Not to be used during pregnancy by epileptics or by people with high blood pressure.

## JASMINE

*Aphrodisiac, antidepressant, a sensual stimulant, warming.*

**Aroma:** Rich, sweet and fruity.

**Therapeutic Benefits:** Mood enhancer, relieves tension, anxiety, depression, fear, lethargy, frigidity impotence, menstrual pains and cramps; dry, sensitive and irritated skin; eases labour during childbirth, relieves post-natal depression (CBM, B, NI, VP).

*Other Uses:* In perfume, cosmetics, herbal teas, room fresheners.

*Caution:* Do not use in the early stages of pregnancy.

## JUNIPER

*Stimulating, refreshing, invigorating, astringent, diuretic, antiseptic, detoxifying, cleansing.*

**Aroma:** Pine-like, smoky woody scent.

**Therapeutic Benefits:** Effective for urinary tract infections, cystitis, oedema (water retention), cellulitis, colic, coughs; aids elimination and relieves flatulence, rheumatism, gout, arthritis; stimulates circulation and appetite, useful for acne, dermatitis, eczema, skin ulcers (SL, CR), psoriasis, (NI, B, CBM), haemorrhoids, exhaustion, confusion.

**Other Uses:** Ingredient of gin, in incense for the sick room.

**Caution:** Avoid during pregnancy.

## LAVENDER

*Calming, soothing, balancing/normalizing, antiseptic, analgesic, antibiotic, anti-depressant, antibacterial, decongestant, sedative, bactericidal, anti-inflammatory, fungicidal.*

**Aroma:** Herby, flowery scent.

**Therapeutic Benefits:** Balances and soothes nervous and emotional exhaustion, headaches, migraine, skin conditions, acne, eczema; infections of the lungs, colds, coughs, catarrh, sinusitis (SI), aids digestion and the urinary tract, vertigo, fainting (NI), serious burns, promotes rapid healing and prevents scarring; effective sedative, combats insomnia; pain relief sciatica, arthritis, rheumatism muscular pain (LM, B); menstruation, scanty periods, reduces high blood pressure, athlete's foot, ringworm, hysteria, manic depression, depression, anxiety (CBM, B, VP).

**Other Uses:** In perfumery, pot-pourri and as an insect repellent (moths).

## LEMON

*Refreshing, highly astringent and antiseptic, a disinfectant and anti-bacterial.*

**Aroma:** Sharp, citrus-fresh scent.
**Therapeutic Benefits:** Used for skin complaints, oily or greasy skin, spots, boils, corns, warts, veruccas; lowers blood pressure; relieves colds, sore throats, digestive problems, fever, gall-stones (SI, B, LM); tonic for circulatory system, mobilizes white blood cells and healing to external wounds, cuts, bruises, insect stings; reduces temperature in flu; counteracts acidity; rheumatism, gout, arthritis, bronchitis.
**Other Uses:** In insect repellents and cooking.
**Caution:** May cause skin irritation (use only 1 per cent in massage oil).

## LEMON-GRASS

*Invigorating, refreshing, energizing, tonic, powerfully antiseptic and anti-bacterial, deodorizing.*

**Aroma:** Refreshing lemony smell.
**Therapeutic Benefits:** Skin complaints, sore throats, respiratory problems, soothes headaches (SI, LM), tones heart and digestive system, is a gastric stimulant; useful in feverish illnesses.
**Other Uses:** In soaps, perfumes, cleaning agents, cooking, insect repellents; protects animals from fleas and tics.
**Caution:** May cause skin irritation (use only 1 per cent in massage oil).

## MARJORAM

*Warming, stimulating, analgesic, sedative, antispasmodic, anaphrodisiac.*

**Aroma:** Warm, penetrating and spicy.
**Therapeutic Benefits:** Use to relieve asthma, bronchitis, colds (SI); relieves spasm and circulatory problems. Useful for treating high blood pressure (CBM), rheumatism, arthritis, stiff joints, tired and painful muscles; encourages menstruation and eases menstrual cramps (HC), constipation, headaches, loneliness and grief, anxiety and insomnia (B).
**Other Uses:** Cooking.
**Caution:** Can cause drowsiness, dull the senses and deaden emotions. Do not use during early pregnancy.

## MELISSA

*Uplifting, anti-depressant, antispasmodic, soothing and calming.*

**Aroma:** Light lemony scent.
**Therapeutic Benefits:** Skin problems such as eczema, allergies; asthma, colds, coughs (SI); regulating effect on menstruation, diarrhoea; lowers high blood pressure, aids migraine, stress headaches, nausea; uplifts mood – induces joy and dispels melancholy, releases tension, grief, shock and bereavement (NI, B, CBM).
**Other Uses:** In room perfumes, insect repellents, distilling liqueurs, cooking.
**Caution:** Can cause skin irritation, (use only in 1 per cent dilution in a massage oil and 3–4 drops in a bath). Avoid during pregnancy.

## MYRRH

*Antiseptic, rejuvenating, anti-inflammatory, fungicidal, expectorant, astringent.*

**Aroma:** Warm, smoky, bitter scent.
**Therapeutic Benefits:** Skin conditions such as eczema, athlete's foot, cracked and chapped skin, mouth ulcers, gum disorders; chest infections, catarrh, chronic bronchitis, colds, sore throats (LM-chest, neck, SI); for digestive problems such as diarrhoea (LM-stomach, abdomen); helps candida (thrush) (D).
**Other Uses:** In perfume, incense, medicine, toothpaste, mouthwash.
**Caution:** Do not use during pregnancy.

## NEROLI

*Rejuvenating, uplifting, anti-depressant, antiseptic, antispasmodic, aphrodisiac, mildly sedative, relaxing.*

**Aroma:** Bitter-sweet, intoxicating orange-blossom scent.
**Therapeutic Benefits:** Calms the emotions, anxiety, shock, hysteria; combats insomnia (B); skin care – all skin types, dermatitis, dry skin (CR, SL); useful for chronic diarrhoea, premenstrual tension, menopause problems (LM-lower abdomen, B).
**Other Uses:** In perfume (Eau-de-Cologne), bridal wreaths.

## ORANGE

*Refreshing, anti-depressant, antispasmodic, mildy sedative.*

**Aroma:** Fresh and sweet.
**Therapeutic Benefits:** Stimulates the digestive system, effective help for constipation, chronic diarrhoea; combats insomnia (VP), mouth ulcers; tonic for anxiety and depression (CBM, B).
**Other Uses:** In perfume, liqueur (Curaçao) food and cosmetic products, confectionery.
**Caution:** In excessive dosage can cause skin irritation.

## PATCHOULI
*Anti-inflammatory, stimulating, tonic, antiseptic, aphrodisiac, sedative.*
**Aroma:** Sweet, woody, musky scent.
**Therapeutic Benefits:** Reduces fever; skin care, acne, eczema, scars, cracked skin, allergies; scalp conditions including dandruff, athlete's foot; alleviates fluid retention (oedema); reduces appetite; uplifting effect in depression and anxiety (CBM, NI, B).
**Other Uses:** In perfume (fixative), incense, insecticides, for treating snake bite and stings from poisonous insects.

## PEPPERMINT
*Cooling/warming, refreshing, invigorating, antispasmodic, stimulating, mildly antiseptic, decongestant.*
**Aroma:** Strong, tangy, refreshing.
**Therapeutic Benefits:** Remedy for digestive upsets, colic, diarrhoea, flatulence, indigestion; relieves nausea

and vomiting, sea and travel sickness, stomach pain (T, LM-stomach, abdomen, B); relieves colds and flu; cools fever, induces sweating (SI); can be used as a skin tonic. (Use only a 1 per cent dilution), controls bacteria causing acne, headache, migraine (CC), catarrh, relieves hot flushes, clears mental fatigue, shock.
**Other Uses:** In toothpaste, medicines, cosmetics, confectionery, insect and vermin control.
**Caution:** Use no more than 3 drops in a bath for people with sensitive skins. Do not use if taking homeopathic remedies. Avoid during pregnancy and whilst breast-feeding.

## PETITGRAIN
*Refreshing, deodorant.*
**Aroma:** Fresh, light flowery scent similar to neroli.
**Therapeutic Benefits:** Very similar to Neroli, but less sedative and stimulating. Excellent bath oil
**Other Uses:** As a flavouring in food and drink.

## PINE
*Refreshing, powerfully antiseptic, deodorant, stimulating.*
**Aroma:** Strong and resinous.
**Therapeutic Benefits:** For treatment of chest infections, colds, bronchitis, catarrh, sinusitis, sore throats (SI); stimulates circulation; relieves rheumatic, arthritic and muscular pain (B, LM); relieves cystitis.

**Other Uses:** In bath preparations, cleaning products, disinfectants, room deodorizers.
**Caution:** Can cause irritation if used neat in a bath; should only be used as part of a blend in massage oil.

## ROSE
*Cleansing, purifying, regulating, tonic, soothing, astringent, a potent anti-depressant, aphrodisiac, antiseptic, mood enhancer.*
**Aroma:** Romantic and feminine.
**Therapeutic Benefits:** Relieves tension, depression, sadness; best remedy for treating disorders of the female reproductive system, regulates the menstrual cycle; relieves post-natal depression, grief, anorexia nervosa, frigidity, impotence; skin care (all skin types), older drier skins; helps circulatory problems, constipation, headaches, mental fatigue. (B, FM).
**Other Uses:** In cosmetics, food preparations, pot-pourri. Caution: avoid during pregnancy.

## ROSEMARY
*Stimulating, strengthening, invigorating, antiseptic, warming, penetrating, tonic, analgesic.*
**Aroma:** Powerful, woody and warm.
**Therapeutic Benefits:** As a sensory restorative, brain stimulant; improves memory, multiple sclerosis; lowers cholesterol; low blood pressure; useful for colds, catarrh, bronchitis, sinusitis, asthma (SI,VP, LM), headaches,

rheumatism, arthritis (B, LM, HC), diarrhoea, flatulence, obesity, overworked muscles; for skin and hair care, alopecia, dandruff (SM).
**Other Uses:** In Eau de Cologne, cooking, shampoo.
**Caution:** Avoid if epileptic, suffering from high blood pressure, pregnant, or taking homeopathic medicines.

## SAGE
*Very stimulating, warming, penetrative.*
**Aroma:** Fresh spicy fragrance.
**Therapeutic Benefits:** Regulates menstruation; relieves arthritis, bacterial infections, water retention; helps muscular aches and prolonged stress (B).
**Other Uses:** Cooking.
**Caution:** Can provoke epileptic fits, uterine spasm and haemorrhage. Use in low dilutions and avoid during early pregnancy.

## SANDALWOOD
*Powerful urinary antiseptic, sedative, aphrodisiac, expectorant, antispasmodic.*
**Aroma:** Sweet, warm and woody.
**Therapeutic Benefits:** Relieves cystitis, dry persistent and irritating coughs, chronic bronchitis, sore throats (SI, LM-chest), dry and dehydrated skins (WC), oily skins and acne, anxiety, nervous tension, depression (CMB, NI,VP).
**Other Uses:** In perfume, incense, toiletries, cosmetics.

## TEA TREE
*Strong disinfectant and antiseptic, cooling, effectively anti-viral, bactericide, fungicide, stimulates immune system, deodorant.*
**Aroma:** Strong, medicinal, eucalyptus-like scent.
**Therapeutic Benefits:** Relieves colds, flu, infectious childhood illnesses (B), cold sores (NA), blisters of shingles and chicken pox, veruccae, warts (NA); for treating skin complaints, acne; fungal infections such as ringworm, athlete's foot, thrush/candida; glandular fever, AIDS (strengthens the immune system), respiratory complaints; catarrh, sinusitis, laryngitis (SI, VP); good for burns, stings, cuts and wounds (their original Aboriginal use), mouth ulcers (as a mouthwash – do not swallow), makes a good deodorizing and antiseptic foot bath.
**Other Uses:** Kills fleas on pets.
**Caution:** Can cause skin irritation so use only 3 drops in a bath.

## THYME
*Stimulating, strengthening, invigorating, balancing, powerfully antiseptic and disinfectant, diuretic.*
**Aroma:** Pungent, sweet and herby.
**Therapeutic Benefits:** Digestive stimulant, intestinal antiseptic, expels worms, round worm, thread worm, tapeworm; natural antiseptic for colds, coughs, sore throats, mouth and gum infections (G); useful for chest

infections (SI), urinary tract infections, stimulates production of white blood corpuscles, raises low blood pressure, stimulates appetite; good for sores, wounds and swellings (CC, HC), rheumatism (HC), insect bites, and stings (CC, B); combats infectious diseases (VP), fatigue, anxiety, lethargy, depression; stimulates brain and improves memory, insomnia (CBM,B).
**Other Uses:** In cooking, toothpaste, mouthwash, colognes, herbal perfumes, incense.
**Caution:** Do not use on anyone suffering from high blood pressure. Do not use on pregnant women or on children's skin. Do not use neat on the skin, always dilute well for a bath.

## YLANG YLANG
*Antidepressant, sedative, aphrodisiac, antiseptic, balancing, tonic.*
**Aroma:** Heavy, sweet and exotic.
**Therapeutic Benefits:** Sedating and regulating effect on the nervous system, shock, fright, stress, anxiety, depression, insomnia; reduces high blood pressure; for facial and skin care – both dry and oily (CBM, B, NI, VP).
**Other Uses:** Perfume, cosmetics, pot-pourri.
**Caution:** Do not use in high concentrations or over a long period of time – it can lead to headaches and nausea. Can irritate sensitive skin.

### KEY TO A–Z OF TREATMENT

**CBM**=Complete Body Massage
**LM**=Local Massage/Rub
**FM**=Facial Massage      **SM**=Scalp
                           Massage
**NA**=Neat Application     **CR**=Cream
**SL**=Skin Lotion         **BS**=Body
                           Scrub
**B**=Bath                 **HB**=Hot Bath
**NB**=Night-time Baths    **SI**=Steam
                           Inhalation
**NI**=Neat Oil Inhalation **G**=Gargle
**CC**=Cold Compress       **HC**=Hot
                           Compress
**WC**=Warm Compress       **GD**=Gauze
                           Dressing
**D**=Douche               **T**=Tea/Tisane
**MDR**=Medical
    Diagnosis Required
**ST**=Skin Test           **VP**=Vaporizer

I love nothing better than going out to buy my essential oils and massage components. Just smelling and testing them gives me a lift. These are my basic guidelines for buying, storing and preparing oils.

## BUYING

1 Buy the best possible organic oils from a reputable company for the very best results. Cheap oils are a false economy. Look for 'pure essential oil' on the label, not 'essence'.

2 Check they are environmentally friendly, non-animal tested and produced solely from plants and their by-products.

3 Certificates of purity are available on request. A reputable company will guarantee pure and economical products, e.g. Neal's Yard of Covent Garden, London.

4 Don't be taken in by fancy packaging.

5 If you find all your oils are a uniform colour then they are not pure oils. They should also vary in price from one to another.

6 Smell essential oils by testing on a handkerchief. If the smell evaporates quickly it is not a pure essential oil. Cultivate your natural intuition and senses to help you buy the best. It is possible to train your sense of smell and touch.

7 Don't be afraid to question the retailer and ask for written information on the products.

8 Test oils for texture. If it is too viscous and spreads on your skin leaving an oily residue then it has had a vegetable oil added to it.

## STORING

1 Keep tightly sealed to prevent evaporation and deterioration through oxidation.

2 Store in a cool dark place with no direct sunlight and an even temperature.

3 Plastic bottles will only keep oils for up to eight weeks. Use dark brown or blue glass bottles.

4 Keep out of the reach of children and animals. Most of these oils are highly toxic if ingested.

5 Most oils except sandalwood, cedarwood, vetiver, patchouli and rose otto (attar of roses) can be stored in a fridge.

6 Most essential oils have a shelf life of about two years if kept in their pure state, i.e. unblended. They tend to go cloudy as they deteriorate. Citrus oils have a six month shelf life, so buy in smaller quantities. Bergamot lasts well, neroli for up to one year, while patchouli and myrrh actually seem to improve with age.

## WHAT YOU NEED

1 A small measuring/dispensing jug (from chemists) and a 5ml medicine-spoon for accurately measuring carrier oils.

2 A glass eye-dropper to dispense essential oils.

3 A glass container or glazed ceramic bowl for mixing (optional).

4 Wooden or ceramic implements (miniature spatula, spoon etc.) for stirring/blending (optional).

5 Dark-tinted glass bottles for storage.
6 Self-adhesive labels and permanent (oil-proof) marker/pen for labelling formulas and partner identification.
7 Folder/index in which to record partner's health records, treatment details and progress.

### PREPARING A MASSAGE OIL AND ESTIMATING QUANTITIES

A standard 5ml medicine-dispensing spoon (freely available) holds exactly 100 drops of oil. Most essential oils are used in a 3 per cent solution. This means three drops of essential oil should be added to a 5ml spoon of chosen carrier oil(s). Obviously one spoonful is not enough for an average adult massage. I would therefore recommend the following proportions:

a) Baby (up to 6 months old, average size) = 1 drop of essential oil to 5ml of a light carrier oil.
b) Child (up to 8 years old, average size) = 2 drops of essential oil to 10ml.
c) Child (from 8–14 years old, average size) = 3 drops of essential oil to 10ml.
c) Adult (small) = 6 drops of essential oil to 10ml.
d) Adult (medium) = 7–8 drops of essential oil to 15ml.
d) Adult (large) = 9–10 drops of essential oil to 20ml.
   If you run out of the blended treatment oil, then supplement it with as much plain carrier oil as required.

### PREPARING A MASSAGE OIL

**Step 1** Check Aromatherapy Guidelines & DON'Ts and DOs (pages 36/38).
**Step 2**
Choose appropriate:
a) Carrier Oil(s)
b) Essential Oils (see A–Z Natural Treatment Charts, pages 69–74)
c) Quantities (see above)
**Step 3** Wash and rinse your hands in clean running water, scrub nails thoroughly and dry on a clean towel. Ideally, nails should be short and polish-free.
**Step 4** Working on a clean, stain-resistant surface, measure required quantity of carrier oil(s) into the dispensing jar or 5ml medicine-spoon. Using an eye dropper, add prescribed number of drops of essential oil(s). Check smell and test texture of oils before using in case they have combined with oxygen and have turned rancid, hardened or lost their freshness. Mix with wooden spatula.
**Step 5** Decant into a clean dark-tinted bottle and shake gently to blend.
**Step 6** Pour into a warmed glazed ceramic bowl, clam shell or similar, and warm your hands in preparation.

### PREPARING A MASSAGE LOTION FOR FACE OR BODY

For those people who prefer the feel of a lotion rather than a vegetable-based oil or are allergic or sensitive to certain products, a hypo-allergenic, non-perfumed, lanolin-free lotion can be used as a base. Proceed as above.

### PREPARING A COMPRESS

**Hot Compress** (to treat pain of a chronic nature).
**Step 1** Fill a basin with two pints of water (as hot as your hands can bear).
**Step 2** Add essential oil(s) to the water. Note: 4–5 drops for adults and 1–2 drops for babies and people with sensitive skins.
**Step 3** Fold a piece of clean, absorbent fabric (lint, cheesecloth, unmedicated cotton wool, clean old sheeting, towelling etc.) and soak in the water, ensuring surface oils are captured.
**Step 4** Wring out excess water and place on affected area.
**Step 5** Remove and replace with a fresh compress when cooled to blood heat.
**Cold Compress** (to treat acute pain and as first-aid for injuries and sprains). Proceed as for hot compress, except that the water should be as cold as possible – preferably cooled with ice. Compresses should be renewed once they have warmed to blood temperature.
**Alternative:** This can take the form of a cream mixture (oats, ground almonds, 4 drops of essential oil in a carrier oil).

## WAYS TO USE ESSENTIAL OILS IN YOUR HOME

### MASSAGE

Aromatherapy possesses a special therapeutic quality. Unlike other forms of massage the essential oils are blended to suit the need of each individual in order to treat them physically, mentally, emotionally and spiritually. It can be enjoyed by all from babies to the very elderly, and is one of the most relaxing ways of enjoying the power of essential oils. They are worked into the body using a variety of techniques which can invigorate and stimulate, revitalize, tone and condition, relax, relieve, soothe, comfort, strengthen and regulate or cleanse and detoxify. This gentle form of massage is a 'treatment' which affects the lymphatic system while the aromas stimulate the emotional centre (i.e. the limbotic system in the brain). It is a valuable way of helping ourselves and others to achieve and maintain the best possible health.

The easy step-by-step instructions shown in this book will teach you the value of give-and-take as well as creating an equilibrium that is rooted in refining and restoring all the senses, especially the sense of smell. It should be as therapeutic for you, the masseur, as it is for your partner.

### BODY SCRUBS

This is an excellent alternative to a traditional aromatherapy massage. My home recipe works wonders on the skin, having the added bonus of improving the circulation. It removes dead cells leaving the skin very smooth and silky.

> **Recipe**
> 2 tablespoons wild oats,
> 2 tablespoons chopped nuts,
> 2 tablespoon ground almonds,
> grated rind of an orange
> bound together with almond
> oil (approx 2–3 tablespoons)
> and 1 drop each of pine,
> eucalyptus, geranium and
> rosewood essential oils.

### STEAM INHALATION

This is not suitable for asthma sufferers, but works wonders for colds and flu, congestion, sinusitis and revitalizing the skin.

> **Recipe**
>
> Add 6 drops of appropriate essential oil(s) to a bowl of very hot water and place on a table. Sit with your head a comfortable distance from the bowl and cover both head and bowl with a large towel to keep the vapour in. Breathe deeply through your nose until the scent has almost disappeared. Repeat up to three times a day. Alternatively, sprinkle a few drops of oil onto a handkerchief (3–4 drops for children) and inhale or sprinkle onto a pillow for a good night's sleep.

Treatments can relieve a wide variety of ailments such as insomnia, tension, sore muscles, poor circulation, period problems, coughs, colds, headaches and fluid retention. Add 6–8 drops of essential oil to a hot bath, lie back, relax and breathe deeply for 2–3 minutes. Remain in the warm water for at least 20 minutes.

### SAUNAS
Sprinkle a few drops of the appropriate oil(s) into the water bucket and let them evaporate over hot coals.

### BATHS
Bathing in essential oils is the perfect way to unwind after a tiring or stressful day. It is a good alternative for people whose skin is too sensitive or painful to tolerate massage. It can help relieve both minor and serious aches and pains and generally soothe and condition the skin. Hand and foot baths are the best preparation for a pedicure, manicure or reflexology treatment. Note: Change the temperature of your bath according to the treatment you need, e.g. if the body is overheating through illness or disease then it is better to have a cooler bath. If you are soaking in a treatment bath, do not use soap or other bath products.

Oils such as pine and eucalyptus are extremely good cleansers and detoxifiers.

## COMPRESSES

Compresses are an effective way of relieving pain and swelling and reducing inflammation. Generally, hot compresses are used to treat chronic pain (backache, fibrositis, rheumatic and arthritic pain, abscesses, earache and toothache) and cold compresses for acute pain and as first-aid for injuries and sprains (headaches, tennis elbow). See page 28 for method of preparation.

## ROOM FRESHENERS

Vaporizers: These can take the form of a ceramic holder consisting of a two-part set. The lower part holds the burner (nightlight candles) and the upper, the vaporizing bowl. Fill the bowl with 2 tablespoons of water and add 2–3 drops of essential oil(s). Place over the nightlight and the aroma will very quickly permeate a room or mask unwelcome smells.

### Ring Burners

Alternatively, place a few drops of your favourite essential oil on a ceramic burner. This simple little device sits on top of a light bulb and gives off a strong aroma as the oil evaporates. Both burners and vaporizers are healthier alternatives to smoky incense and artificial air fresheners and sprays.

### Pot-pourri

Dry your own leaves, petals and slices of fruit and peel and soak with a few drops of essential oil in a wooden or ceramic container. Bought oil-scented, hand-carved fruit are an attractive alternative option for scenting a room.

### Shells, Pine Cones, Stones

Brush them with your favourite oil and display them on the soil in plant pots or on shelves.

### Scented Candles

Candles made from pure essential oils are readily available, but check carefully that they contain genuine ingredients.

An aromatic bath can be extremely versatile: it can be used to relax and sedate or uplift and stimulate. However, more importantly, it is the stress-reducing properties that are most in demand. An additional 'treatment' such as this can be used in between sessions with your aromatherapist or as part of a self-help programme. Fill your bath with hot water, keeping all the doors and windows closed when the bath is full. Add 6 drops of your chosen essential oil(s) and disperse with your hand. Then just simply relax in the warm perfumed water for at least 20 minutes.

**For children:** (between 5–12 years old). Use only 3–4 drops of essential oils blended with 5ml of a light carrier oil.

**For babies:** All essential oils (2 drops only) must be blended first with 5ml of skimmed milk or carrier oil (sunflower or soya).

**For sensitive or dry skin:** Use a blend with 5ml of carrier/dispersing oil.

**Caution:** Do not use any of the following bath preparation when pregnant.

### REFRESHING BATH
*to ease colds, coughs, exhaustion, tired over-worked muscles*
pine (2 drops), juniper (2 drops), basil (2 drops)

### INVIGORATING & STIMULATING BATH
*to ease poor circulation*
basil (2 drops), patchouli (2 drops), juniper or rosemary (2 drops)
**Caution:**
Do not use if suffering from high blood pressure.

### REVITALIZING BATH
*to ease aches, pains, tired muscles, regulate menstruation and alleviate water retention*
eucalyptus (3 drops), rosemary (3 drops), sage (1 drop)
**Caution:**
Do not use if suffering from high blood pressure.

### RELAXING BATH
*to ease stress, tension, insomnia, anxiety, shock, hysteria*
camomile (4 drops), lavender (2 drops),
*or*
neroli (2 drops), rose (2 drops), jasmine (2 drops)

### RELIEVING BATH
*to relieve psoriasis, dermatitis, eczema, shingles, cystitis, stress*
bergamot (2 drops), eucalyptus (2 drops), tea-tree (2 drops)
or to relieve depression, high blood pressure
lavender (3 drops), bergamot (3 drops)

### SOOTHING BATH
*to soothe arthritis, rheumatism, headaches, shock, anger, anxiety*
lavender (3 drops), camomile (3 drops)

### COMFORTING BATH
*to soothe constipation, indigestion, stress*
petitgrain (3 drops), lavender (2 drops), rose (1 drop)

### STRENGTHENING & INVIGORATING
*to regulate high and low blood pressure, and ease colds, flu, bronchitis*
geranium (2 drops), thyme (2 drops), black pepper (1 drop)
*or*
lavender (3 drops), camomile (3 drops)

### CLEANSING & DETOXIFYING
*to ease hangovers, overweight, flatulence, sinusitis, catarrh*
Blend any three of the following:
juniper (2 drops), fennel (2 drops), lavender (2 drops), lemon (2 drops), orange (2 drops), sandalwood (2 drops)

### APHRODISIAC
*to ease frustration, headaches, migraine*
jasmine (5 drops), black pepper (1 drop)
*or*
neroli (2 drops), bergamot (1 drop), ylang ylang (3 drops)

## DON'Ts

*Contra-indications that will help you avoid mistakes in choosing oils, make a basic health assessment of your partner, and help you observe important safety guidelines*

1  Acupuncture: A treatment is not to be given if your partner has had acupuncture on the same day.

2  Alcohol: Do not treat anyone with substantial amounts of alcohol in their system. Also, be sure to advise your partner not to indulge for at least six hours after a treatment if they wish it to be effective.

3  Asthma: Do not treat advanced cases.

4  Baths: Do not treat anyone who has had a hot bath immediately prior to treatment. A warm shower or bath is advised.

5  Blood Pressure (high): Do not use rosemary.

6  Cuts, Swellings, Sprains: Do not massage over them.

7  Cancer: Give only gentle hand and face treatments where appropriate.

8  Deodorants: Ask your partner to refrain from using deodorants or body preparations if they are planning to have a treatment.

9  Driving: Advise your partner to refrain from driving or using machinery if they feel at all drowsy after their treatment.

10  Eating: Do not treat you partner if they have eaten within the previous

two hours or have had a drink during the last half an hour as it may cause indigestion

11  Energy Levels: Do not give a treatment if your energy levels are low or you have a cold or flu.

12  Epilepsy: Do not use rosemary, hyssop, sweet fennel or sage.

13  Heart Conditions: Do not treat advanced cases.

14  Heat: Advise your partner to refrain from exposing his or her body to heat from hair dryers, sunbeds or saunas for at least six hours after a treatment.

15  Hyperthyroidism: Do not treat without medical advice.

16  Inoculation: Do not treat anyone who has had an inoculation within the previous three weeks.

17  Internal Use: Although acceptable in the form of commercially available teas, it is generally not recommended for anyone other than a trained aromatherapist to advise any preparation to be taken by mouth.

18  Operations: Do not treat anyone who has had an operation within the previous six months.

19  Periods: Do not give a treatment to anyone during their period. You can use sedating oils, not stimulating oils, for two days either side of the period itself.

20  Pregnancy: There are certain oils which must be avoided in various stages of pregnancy. Without advice from a qualified aromatherapist, avoid

the following altogether: aniseed, armoise, arnica, basil, birch, camomile, camphor, cedarwood, clary sage, cypress, fennel, hyssop, jasmine, juniper, lavender, marjoram, myrrh, origanum, pennyroyal, peppermint, rose, rosemary, sage, savory, thyme, wintergreen, plus any other oil with toxic properties.

21 Sunbathing: Advise your partner to refrain from sunbathing on the same day as their treatment if you use citric oil or a high proportion of bergamot in the blend. These contain tanning agents and can affect the pigmentation of the skin.

22 Thrombosis: Do not treat anyone with thrombosis.

Note: If you or your partner disregard any of the above guidelines, the treatment will not only be less effective but could be dangerous in certain circumstances. If in any doubt about ANY medical condition, PLAY IT SAFE and consult a medical practitioner or trained aromatherapist before commencing a treatment. Ultimately it is up to you to use your common sense and discretion as to how far these guidelines may be broken. Best of all, get yourself properly trained!

## DOs

*How to choose the appropriate oils, make a basic health assessment of your partner, and be aware of some important safety guidelines*

1   Blood Pressure (high): Massage should be given with a much lighter touch than normal. Do not use rosemary essential oil.

2   Body Conditions: Take note of the following factors and observations to help you choose the most appropriate oils for treatment:

a)   dietary problems (i.e. diabetes, overweight, underweight, anorexia nervosa, bulimia, ulcers, colitis, constipation, flatulence, diarrhoea, indigestion).

b)   muscle tone and texture (i.e. tense, relaxed, contracted, tender, unconditioned. Be particularly careful where there is a heart condition).

c)   skin type (i.e. dry, oily, sensitive cracked, irritated, inflamed, blotchy).

d)   circulation (i.e. sluggish, poor)

e)   the spine (i.e. curvature, distortion, spondylosis).

f)   joints (i.e. stiff, inflamed, painful, inflexible, swollen).

g)   systems under stress (i.e. nervous, muscular, digestive, skeletal, circulatory, urinary, respiratory etc.)

h)   mind and emotions (i.e. stress/tension, depression, anxiety, grief, loneliness, fear, anger, apathy, lethargy, oversensitivity, trauma, lack of concentration, shock, addiction, insecurity, lack of confidence).

3   Epilepsy: Seizures may be controlled with ylang ylang, lavender and camomile.

4   Energy Levels: Check your partner's energy levels (i.e. overactive, busy, calm, tired, irritable, low).

5   General State of Health: Query your partner's general state of health (i.e. robust, healthy, poor, unhealthy) and, if you can without prying, find reasons, i.e. physical factors such as infections, colds, flu, sinusitis etc., problems in a relationship/family, school, work etc.

6   Homeopathic Remedies: If your partner is taking homeopathic remedies, ask them to check with their practitioner before using essential oils.

7   Hydration: It is most important to hydrate the system after an aromatherapy treatment. Please offer your partner a drink of water after treatment and encourage them to drink more water to help the process.

8   Medication: Take into account any medication being taken by your partner as it can have adverse effects when combined with aromatherapy. Consult a medical practitioner.

9   Mental and Physical Handicap: Partners with handicaps can be treated very successfully provided you reduce any formula to half strength at first increasing it when you feel it is safe.

10  **Sleep Patterns:** Find out if your partner is sleeping well, cannot sleep (insomnia), has difficulty getting to sleep, is waking early or waking unrefreshed.

11  Safety:

a)   Keep oils out of the way of children and animals; many are toxic in their concentrated forms.

b)   Screw tops tightly on bottles after use and keep in a cool, dark, place away from sunlight.

c)   Wipe any spillages from working surfaces to avoid staining.

d)   Keep oils away from eyes (note: never massage within the orbits of your partner's eyes: in case of accident, wash in a weak saline solution, seeking medical advice if irritation persists).

e)   Remove jewellery (except wedding bands) during treatments.

f)   Only use prescribed amounts of blended oils as they are very potent. If you run out, supplement with as much additional carrier oil as required.

12  Time: Allow up to one and a half hours for treatment and be sure your partner rests quietly on their own for 10-15 minutes after they have been made comfortable and warm.

13  Treatment: Prepare for treatment (refer to page 40) and attend to the important little details as they will be appreciated by your partner.

14  Young Children: Children to 7 years – use diluted quantities of essential oils in the bath, i.e. 1–2 drops in 5ml of a light carrier oil.

## Preparing the Environment

**Step 1** Make sure there are no interruptions or distractions during the session together. Switch off the phone or put on your answering machine. Allow at least an hour and a half for a full body treatment.

**Step 2** Play background music suitable to the mood and temperament of your partner. There is a wide range of cassettes/CDs of music and natural sounds specifically composed for this kind of situation (optional).

**Step 3** The treatment area/room should be warm and inviting (at least 70°F/21°C) and, if working on the floor, the room temperature should be higher. Although the room needs to be well-ventilated, there should be no cold draughts.

**Step 4** Artificial lighting should be subdued and indirect and natural light should be filtered, if possible. Lighted candles add a feeling of peace and tranquillity to the atmosphere, even in daylight conditions. However, certain oils are flammable and care needs to be exercised.

**Step 5** Enhance the effectiveness of your treatment by burning complementary oils as a welcome gesture. If you wish, sprinkle the massage bed/table with the leaves of freshly picked herbs or flowers.

**Step 6** Use only cotton or linen sheets and warm three bath towels before covering your partner's body. Where necessary, place rolled cotton sheets under knees, ankles, neck or forehead for comfortable support. Have a warmed blanket ready to cover your partner during the rest period at the end of the treatment. The more thought and effort you put into making your partner comfortable, the more cherished they will feel and the greater the benefit they are likely to derive from the treatment.

## Preparing Yourself

**Step 7** Have a warm shower with a body scrub (loofah or mitt) using unperfumed products to avoid any unpleasant clash of odours. Any conflict between your own perfume and the treatment oils could easily prove offensive to your partner. Tie back loose hair, wear comfortable, loose-fitting clothes in soothing colours. Bare feet are optional. Note: It may be stating the obvious, but do check that you, yourself, do not have any allergic or adverse reactions to the range of oils that you are likely to use in treatment.

**Step 8** Check through your massage techniques in order to hold them uppermost in your mind during the treatment (see pages 42–43).

## Preparing Your Partner

**Step 9** Offer a shower to your partner prior to treatment since the skin should be as clean as possible and free from deodorant, body lotion and cosmetics. A body loofahed or scrubbed free of dead skin makes the treatment more effective. Offer them the chance to visit the bathroom before you start the treatment. Ideally, all jewellery and rings should be removed. Request your partner to remove all clothing (especially when doing a full body massage) unless it is very obvious that he or she is extremely self-conscious.

**Step 10** With your partner face down/face up on the bed, cover upper torso, hips and legs with three large, warmed towels.

**Step 11** Check through the important aromatherapy guidelines with your partner (see pages 36–38) to be sure that there are no strong indications against commencing certain treatments. If in any doubt consult a doctor or trained aromatherapist.

**Step 12** Make up a special blend of oils to suit your partner (see A-Z Natural Treatment Charts pages 69–74).

**Step 13** Before you blend them, let your partner smell and approve your selection of treatment oils. Let their

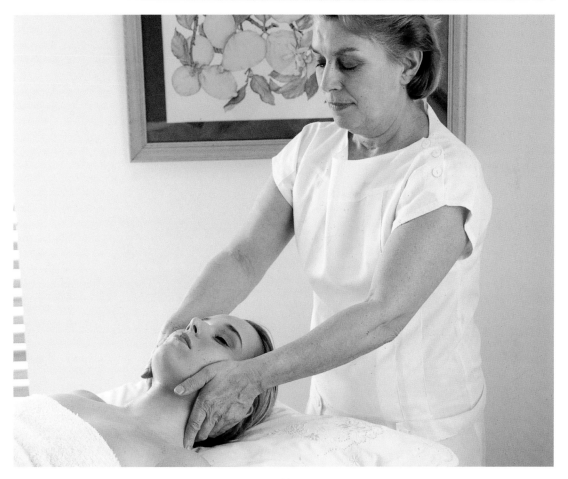

intuition and preferences guide you in your final choice of ingredients. A strong aversion to an oil could well indicate that it would be harmful or inefficacious to this particular person. Prepare your oils (see pages 26–28). Test the blended oils on both your own and your partner's forearm. If irritation or redness appears, substitute or dilute the blend.

Note: A number of factors such as menstruation, stress and certain drugs may heighten sensitivity to this test.

### MASSAGE TECHNIQUES

**Step 14** Perform the cleansing process, The Waterfall. Imagine you are standing beneath a fresh, clear-running waterfall. It washes all over you, removing negative energy and psychic impurities. The imaginary water pools at your feet and flows away harmlessly back to Nature. Then, gently stroke your partner's aura (psychic energy just above the surface of the skin) from head to toe, as if you were drawing away negativity. Shake your hands as if casting it away. Alternatively, flick the energy periodically into a small bowl of sea salt granules. The salt can later be cleansed by standing it in sunlight. I consider these practices to be invaluable and essential preliminaries.

**Step 15** If you think your partner would benefit from a healing thought then suggest one that they can repeat

mentally, during the treatment. You too, can repeat a healing thought: I am an instrument for natural flowing energy (optional).

**Step 16** Now start your aromatherapy massage by gently touching the body through the towel to make physical contact. Some people will have more physical 'armour' than others, so this is a way of breaking down unnecessary barriers.

**Step 17** Uncover the part(s) of the body to receive massage. Remember to replace the coverings after they have been massaged.

**Step 18** Oil your hands, wrists and forearms with carrier oil(s). Warm your hands (by chafing vigorously) and pour a little blended oil into your cupped palm. Rub palms gently together and smooth onto the body. Replenish the oil as required throughout the massage.

**Note:** If you find that your partner's skin is particularly dry, absorbent or hairy and is soaking up so much oil that you think you may not have enough to finish the massage, then add more carrier oil(s) to supplement it. Remember the 'dosage' of essential oils is a calculated 'treatment', so do not make up more blended oils as a replenishment.

**Step 19** Start the massage with a gentle touch and, once you have made contact with your partner, try to keep it flowing until the massage treatment is complete.

**Step 20** Performing each stroke no more than six times (otherwise it can cause irritation), maintain a smooth, slow, gentle pressure throughout. One technique should flow into another, the sixth stroke being a soothing technique such as 'fir tree'. Always work your strokes towards the heart where possible, never drag your movements down.

**Step 21** Keep the fingers slightly parted, palms pressing down onto the body, wrists, elbows and shoulders relaxed. Keep the breath natural, i.e. breathe on impulse. Don't hold your breath, this would indicate you are concentrating too hard. Use deeper pressure for people suffering from depression and a lighter touch for those suffering from high blood pressure. Relax into the movements.

**Step 22** The entire surface of the skin can be covered by moulding your hands to fit the contours over which they are flowing.

**Step 23** Keep the flow going. Don't worry if a particular technique is missed, the very best masseurs work intuitively.

**Step 24** Ease stressed muscles and joints but do not press on bones, vertebrae, behind the knees or on swollen muscles.

**Step 25** Watch out for any cuts or bruises and never massage varicose veins or legs affected with thrombosis (blood clots).

**Step 26** Keep your conversation to a minimum but allow your partner to talk if they need to, even if it is to comment on a particular technique or stroke. If, by any chance, your partner gets upset due to stress release, don't attempt to stop them – crying can encourage the healing process.

**Step 27** Massage with both 'sides' and 'edges' of the hands as well as with wrists and forearms where required.

**Step 28** Use your own weight rather than muscle power to apply pressure.

**Step 29** Pay attention to your posture whether standing, sitting or kneeling. Rock from foot to foot with longer-flowing movements and stay centred within your own sense of inner peace.

**Step 30** Remember, you are massaging a unique living person, not merely skin, flesh and bones. Put yourself in their place from time to time.

**Step 31** Don't be afraid to experiment with your own techniques, this can be a useful and interesting experience. Be open and receptive to new ideas. This is a fascinating subject which is constantly developing and improving.

**Step 32** Encourage feedback at the end of the session so that you can avoid any techniques that your partner did not enjoy or repeat what they did like at a later date.

**Step 33** Invite your partner to reciprocate by giving a treatment themselves at some future date.

AROMATHERAPY AFTERCARE

**Step 34** When the massage is complete, cover your partner with a warmed blanket and tuck them in. Make sure they are comfortable and leave them to rest for at least 10 minutes on their own.

**Step 35** Offer a glass of water (with an optional slice of orange/lemon/lime) to hydrate the system. Encourage them to drink more water during the next few hours. Emphasize the importance of this point.

**Step 36** Advise your client to:
a) refrain from drinking alcohol for up to 6 hours after the treatment (otherwise they might get extremely drunk).

b) avoid heat treatments (such as the use of hairdriers, sunbeds and infra-red appliances) for up to six hours after treatment.

c) allow as many hours as possible for the treatment to take effect before taking a bath or shower (preferably up to 12 hours).

d) wear loose-fitting clothes for as long as possible to allow the skin to breathe freely and to try not to rush around after a treatment.

e) be extra careful if driving or operating machinery due to the possibility of drowsiness after treatment.

WARN YOUR CLIENT ABOUT
THE FOLLOWING

f) Urine may appear darker and stronger-smelling since toxins are often released by the treatment.

g) Headaches can sometimes occur for the same reason.

h) If your partner feels breathless, uses Ventolin for asthma or is taking steroids, they should supplement their diet with vitamins A, D & C.

Helps relieve these physical conditions: fatigue, poor circulation, hypotension, menopause, unconditioned muscles, cellulite. Helps relieve these emotional/mental conditions: depression, apathy, sluggishness, boredom, despondency, grief, bereavement, hopelessness, lethargy, resignation, sadness.

### HEALING AFFIRMATION

Every condition, both physical, emotional and mental can be healed with the appropriate positive healing affirmation. It will help your partner, during this particular massage, if they hold the following image and phrase in their mind during the session (optional): *I am filled with vigour and enthusiasm for life.* If your partner finds this helpful they can safely continue repeating it as often as they wish in their day-to-day life.

### TECHNIQUE

Everyone loves this first step to Aromatherapy massage, especially children. It uses oils that are as near to nature as possible and is a gentle introduction for people who are sensitive about being touched. If practising this technique in the summertime, use very cold oranges straight from the fridge. Lemons, limes and small grapefruit can be used as alternatives (as long as you round off the ends).

**Step 1** Remove stalks and leaves from two oranges (same size).

**Step 2** Prick skins to allow aromatic juices to flow and the smell to fill the air.

**Step 3** Cut open additional fruits and put in a dish nearby to enhance the effect of the aroma.

**Step 4** Ask your partner to lie on their back, arms a little apart from the body, palms uppermost, legs relaxed from the hips, feet apart. Starting at the breastbone (sternum) in the centre of the chest, roll an orange in small circular movements, using palm and fingers, down the left arm, circling into the palm. From there, roll onto the side of the leg (still circling) and down to the left instep. Using the other orange, press into the right instep and circle, working up the side of the leg and into the right palm, circling again. Roll up the arm and finish in the starting position. Try experimenting on the torso with a variety of movements and techniques using one or two oranges; circling, up-and-down, side-to-side, etc.

**Note:** Be gentle around the breasts, ribcage and groin, avoiding neck and face. Work only in a clockwise direction over the areas of the stomach and intestines.

**Step 5** Assist your partner to turn onto their front. Start by circling an orange on the palm of the left hand. With circling motions, roll up one arm then change to 'figure-of-eight' movements around the right and left shoulders. Continue circling down the muscles of the left side of the torso, over the buttock and down the leg (gently over back of the knees). Finish by circling, with slight pressure, into the instep of the foot. Reverse the process. Using the second orange, circle into the right instep, up the leg, over the buttock, up the muscles of the right side of the torso (using 'figure-of-eight' movements round left and right shoulders) and down the right arm, circling into the palm.

**Step 6** The final technique involves gentle pummelling movements (tapping with the fruit) on areas of cellulite, i.e. upper arms, buttocks and thighs. This will help to warm the body in preparation for the aromatherapy massage.

**Step 7** Complete the massage with the oranges resting in your partner's palms. Allow them to rest for 10–15 minutes under a warmed blanket, if necessary.

**Step 8** Serve cool, freshly-squeezed orange juice (sprig of fresh mint optional).

> **General Note:** In winter the massage can be performed over the clothes but, of course, do not prick the fruit skins!

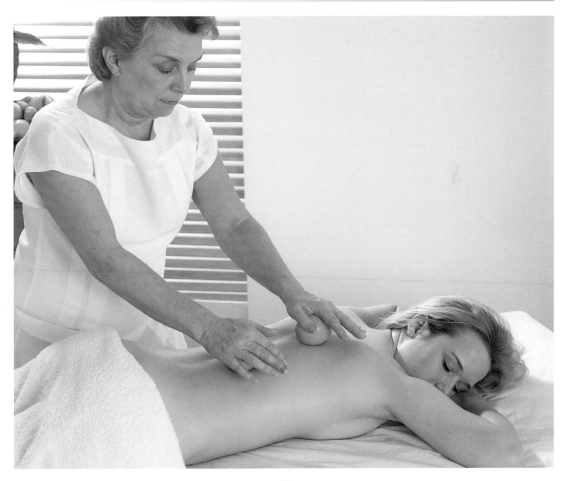

Helps relieve these physical conditions: poor circulation, constipation, obesity, oedema (fluid retention), varicose veins, cramps, arthritis, sexual problems. Helps relieve these emotional/mental conditions: depression, mental fatigue, anger, selfishness, oversensitivity, fear and unforgivingness.

### HEALING AFFIRMATION

It will help your partner, during this particular massage, if they hold the following image and phrase in their mind during the session (optional): *I am free to circulate loving energy to every part of my life.*

There are many different types of overweight people and, as in the case of underweight people, it is necessary to work on the root causes. There are many different types of overweight people. The strong and solid type possess a very powerful presence. They may, however, be so full of uncertainties and unnecessary fears that they feel prevented from expressing their inner power because of its overwhelming effect on others. Often cautious and slow to communicate their own needs, they can suffer a frustrating build-up of suppressed energy which can erupt in outbursts of anger and impatience. The 'flabby' type is often unfocused and uncentred and they tend to waste their precious energy on others. Their muscle tone is an indication of this. There are other overweight types who unconsciously cocoon themselves in

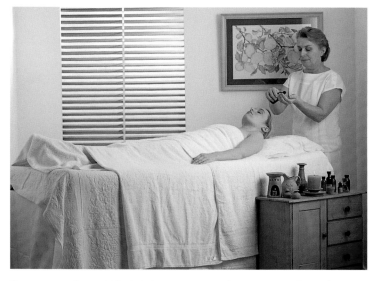

fat as a protection to hide their insecurity. Oversensitive and fearful, they are resistant to change and find it difficult to forgive.

The root cause of all weight imbalance is a breakdown in the equal exchange of incoming and outgoing energies. The key to success is to put your vital energy behind your own truth – a balance will then naturally occur.

### Technique

The most common complaint I hear from people with weight problems is poor circulation. My own method is to work my way up from the roots (feet) towards the emotional centre, heart and head. All the techniques are slow and rhythmical, made with slightly open fingers, wrists relaxed, palms gently pressing over the contours of the body. I use my entire arm from fingertips (both back and front) to wrists, forearms and elbows, where necessary. The feet have nerve endings that are connected to the inner organs by way of energy lines known as meridians. Working on the feet helps to clear blockages and keep the energies flowing.

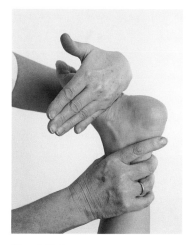

**Step 1** EDGING
Uncover legs, lift the left foot and support it with the right hand. Press the edge of your left hand into the instep and out towards the heel. Repeat six times.

**General Note:** To improve poor circulation, avoid wearing nylon stockings too often as they restrict circulation. Reflexology is an excellent complementary treatment for the feet. It revitalizes the whole body. For more details see pages 62/63.

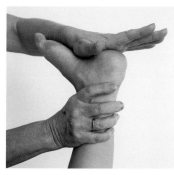

**Step 2** SMOOTHING
Press the palm of your left hand over the sole of the foot, drawing it down from heel to toes. Repeat six times.

**Step 3** PIANO ONE
Walk your nails over the sole of the foot from toes to heel. Repeat six times. Repeat Step 2 (Smoothing) three times.

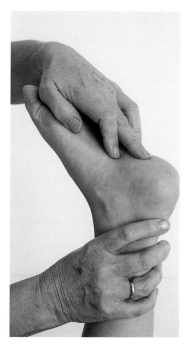

**Step 4** PIANO TWO
Walk your fingertips over the sole of the foot from toes to heel. Repeat six times. Repeat Step 2 (Smoothing) three times.

Repeat steps 1–4 on the right foot.

Helps relieve these physical conditions: underweight, anorexia nervosa, loss of appetite, tautness due to nervous tension. Helps relieve these emotional/mental conditions: overstress, insecurity, anxiety, insomnia, hyperactivity, lack of self-respect, lack of confidence, fear of the future.

### HEALING AFFIRMATION
It will help your partner, during this particular massage if they hold the following image and phrase in their mind during the session (optional): For those who are underweight: *It is safe for me to stand on my own two feet* or *It is safe for me to give and receive love.*

Underweight people tend very often to put all their energy into being something they are not and try desperately to obtain love from others through their own insecurity. They often have physical or emotional symptoms which indicate that they are suffering from excessive stress which they could avoid if they channelled their energies correctly. Characteristically they are tense, taut, thin, hasty, rapid and nervous in their movements, often anxious, possibly hyperactive even though tired. They often have difficulty relaxing and sleeping. Unfortunately, they direct their energy into what they 'perceive' is required of them by others, trying to obtain love by easing someone else's pain. Their energy can easily become depleted since it is being drained into the maintenance of a false idea of themselves. The emotional adjustment they need to make is to learn to respect themselves, to do only

**Step 1** FLUSHING
Right. Stand or sit at your partner's feet. With your hands enfolding the left ankle, work your thumbs up the back of the leg over ankle, calf and thigh. Still with the same long, slow movement, part hands to outer and inner thigh, and bring them back down either side of the leg to the ankle, taking care not to drag. Repeat six times on both legs.

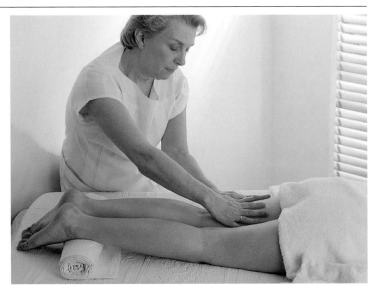

what is best for them (realizing that, eventually, this is what is right for everybody else). They need to realize they can say 'NO' more often. The sense of fear, self-hatred and rejection can, however, be removed by the power of the mind.

Working on the legs may seem a perverse way of correcting the imbalances in underweight people. I find it helps to get to the roots of the problems causing the condition. Basically, any weight imbalance (be it over or underweight) is caused through an imbalance of energy flow in the body, mind and emotions. There are many different types of underweight people whose problems have a variety of root causes. For example, there are those who block the flow of life force or loving energy in denying themselves pleasure. They very often end up with thick legs and aching lower backs. A second cause might be revealed in a glandular imbalance. This can best be relieved by regular yoga-type exercises, deep relaxation, meditation and massage. Fundamentally, there needs to be a balance between the 'incoming energy' (in the form of food or loving energy for instance) and 'outgoing energy' (in the form of daily exercise and emotional output). In whatever way we choose to 'take in' or 'give out', there needs to be a perfect equilibrium. Massage puts us in touch with the rhythm of energies within and around us. It connects us to the root causes of many body, mind and emotional problems and this, as I'm sure you will agree, is the most natural way of solving any problem.

---

**Step 2** LEG EFFLEURAGE
This special technique can be used between each step, using either the heel of the hand or the fingertips (as illustrated). Standing to the left side of your partner, place your left hand on the left ankle. Smooth upwards towards the buttock and slide down to the outer thigh. As the left hand starts to descend the leg the right hand brushes upwards to just above the knee. The left hand crosses over the top of the right to touch the ankle and start again. Repeat six times on each leg.

**Step 3** PICKING UP
Gently pick up the muscles with fingers and thumbs, working from lower calf to thigh. Smooth down with your palms and repeat six times on each leg.

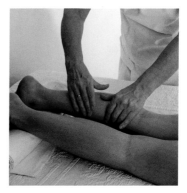

**Caution:** Do not massage back of knees, injuries, swellings, varicose veins or where thrombosis (blood clots) are present.

**General Note:** This needs to be a 'gentle touch' massage. Prepare for the massage (Steps 1–13, page 40/42).

Helps relieve these physical conditions: rounded shoulders, asthma, bronchitis, headache, migraine, fibrositis, high blood pressure. Helps relieve these emotional/mental conditions: anxiety, insomnia, mental exhaustion, nervous tension, lack of confidence, emotional trauma, fear.

### HEALING AFFIRMATION

It will help your partner, during this particular massage, if they hold the following image and phrase in their mind during the session (optional): *I am growing out of my old limitations through the freedom of my creativity.*

A great deal of tension is built up in the back and these special techniques are the most popular part of my aromatherapy treatment. The massage should consist of broad, expansive movements delivered with even pressure, the strokes being aimed at drawing out inflammation and tension by teasing the tight muscles into relaxation. If your partner has suffered back injury due to accident, advise them to consult a medical practitioner (G.P., osteopath, chiropractor, physiotherapist etc.) before applying treatment. In most cases, the relaxing and releasing of muscle tension should be of great benefit.

We are all familiar with the strains of driving and travelling. In the longer term it pays dividends to check that your seat is supporting your back and that the base of the spine is in alignment with the crown of the head, i.e. the base vertebrae should touch the back of the chair, preferably with the chin at right-angles to the chest. Imagine 'growing out of the spine' and expand not just the ribs but the pectoral muscles. This will help relieve some of the tension which builds up in the shoulders through bad posture.

Emotional traumas are often the root cause of backache. The phrase, 'you are a pain in the neck', springs to mind. Whether the so-called cause derives from the unreasonable demands of people near to us or from society in general, tension and fear are stored like recordings in our back muscles. When this kind of problem becomes chronic, leading to rounded shoulders and deformed spines, it is often described as 'carrying the weight of the world on your shoulders'.

### Technique

If your partner is suffering from high blood pressure, use a lighter touch. Prepare for the massage (Steps 1–13, page 40–42).

### Step 1 EFFLEURAGE

(Upside-down 'fir tree' – not illustrated.) Stand or kneel at the head of your partner. Press the fingers either side of the spine at the base of the skull and smooth along the muscles towards the lower back as far as you can comfortably reach. Open hands out and draw palms in and up the sides of the body towards the armpits. Repeat six times to work the oils into the back and sides. Move around to the left side of the body, keeping your right fingertips on the right shoulder. Reinforce with the left hand on top.

### Step 2 NECK-KNEADING

Knead the muscles either side of the neck between thumbs and other fingers. This helps to break up fatty tissues and relieve tension.

**Step 3** SHOULDER FIGURE-OF-EIGHT Right. With one hand on top of the other, give firm effleurage in figure-of-eight around right, then left, shoulder blades. Think: 'palm down, wrist relaxed'. Repeat six times.

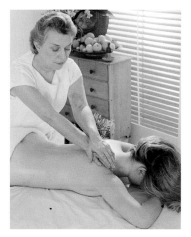

**Step 4** DOUBLE FIGURE-OF-EIGHT Above. Open fingers and rest the uppermost fingers between the lower ones so that all the fingers are resting on the shoulder. Repeat as Step 3 with smooth, flowing strokes.

**General Note:** Correct posture plays an integral part in preventing neck, shoulder and back tension. Practice standing tall, pulling the weight off your ankles, knees and hips. Extend the back of your neck with your chin at right-angles to your chest, shoulders back, down and in. Being aware of how we use and abuse our bodies in everyday movements can form the basis of future corrective exercise. It will be effective only if you appraise yourself regularly and pay attention to what you are doing wrong.

Helps relieve these physical conditions: lumbago, premenstrual tension, menopause, backache. Helps relieve these emotional/mental conditions: deep depression, emotional trauma or upset, fear, anxiety.

### HEALING AFFIRMATION
It will help your partner, during this particular massage, if they hold the following image and phrase in their mind during the session (optional): *I am free to release the past.*

### Technique
In treating the back muscles, always make sure that your partner does not have any misplaced or damaged discs or any damage to the pelvis. If in any doubt recommend they obtain diagnosis and treatment from a good osteopath, chiropractor or physiothera-pist. A qualified yoga teacher will later be able to suggest special remedial exercises to relax, strengthen and tone the back muscles. A great deal of unnecessary pain can be avoided. The draining technique, described here, brings almost instant relief to lumbago. If your partner is low in energy, or deeply depressed, increase the pressure of your touch during massage. Prepare for the massage (Steps 1–13, pages 40–42).

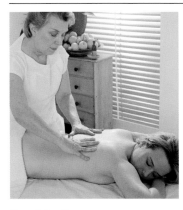

### Step 1 FIR TREE
Place both hands on the lower back, either side of the spine, thumb and forefinger about $1^1/2$ (4cm) apart, to form a 'fir tree' shape. Smooth up the spine and out across the shoulders, gently brushing down the sides to resume the starting position. Repeat six times.

### Step 2 DRAINING
Press the edges of your hands either side of the lower spine, palms facing one another. Press downwards and outwards to the sides, drawing the muscles away from the spine. Bring the right, then left hand, back to the centre a few inches above the starting position and repeat the process until

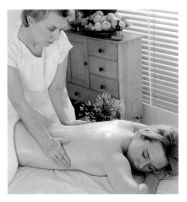

the whole of the back has been 'divided' by this draining stroke. Repeat three times up the spine. Repeat Step 1, Fir Tree, three times as a smoothing stroke – it heralds the end of the draining technique.

### Step 3 THUMB PRESS/RELEASE
Right below. As your partner breathes out, press down on the muscles either side of the spine. Starting at the top of the spine near the shoulder, with thumbs facing each other, smooth down the length of muscle on one side of the spine. Then, again starting at the top of the spine, use the right thumb, closely trailed by the left thumb which presses and releases every 2 inches, to smoothe the muscle using even pressure throughout. On reaching the base of the spine, take the left thumb to the other side at the top of the spine and repeat the process. Repeat on alternate sides twice. Then repeat Step 1, Fir Tree, three times.

**Step 4** PINCHING
Below. Starting under the right armpit, pinch the flesh together using the entire length of your index fingers. Finish just above the waist. Repeat three times on each side. Then repeat Step 1 three times.

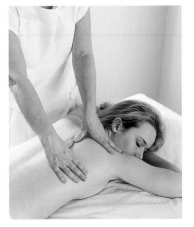

**Step 5** PICKING UP
Above. Pick up the flesh from the side of the torso between the thumb and first two or three fingers. Edge your way gradually down the torso, gently lifting and releasing. Repeat six times. Then repeat Step 1, Fir Tree, three times.

**Step 6** FANNING
Above. Using outward-flowing, 'fanning' movements of the palms and thumbs, work the muscles around the lumbar region. This is especially helpful in relieving premenstrual tension. Repeat six times. Then repeat Step 1, Fir Tree, three times.

**General Note:** To relieve severe depression, encourage your partner to deepen their breathing patterns.

Helps relieve these physical conditions: arthritis, rheumatism, headaches, neuralgia, migraine, premenstrual tension, menopause. Helps relieve these emotional/mental conditions: nervous tension, depression, anxiety, insomnia, shock, stress-related conditions, anger, lack of concentration.

### HEALING AFFIRMATION
It will help your partner, during this particular massage, if they hold the following image and phrase in their mind during the session (optional): For anxiety: *I trust the process of life.* For depression: *Laughter is the melody of my soul*, or *I trust my creative approach to life.*

One of the first things I notice about a student is their hands. If the shoulders are hunched, with the backs of the hands facing forwards I would suspect a depressed state of mind. Clenched fists indicate an angry, closed mind, and is often accompanied by headaches, neuralgia, migraine etc. Constantly fidgeting fingers are a sure indication of a person living on nervous energy and lacking in concentration. Laced fingers against the torso are a sign of a person locked inside their own minds and will often be accompanied by anxiety and depression. Some students simply have problems letting their hands relax, with the result that they find it difficult to let go of their work and are constantly on the 'go'. The most common difficulty a masseur will face is the partner who cannot 'give' their hands in a relaxed way to

them for treatment. This may be caused by an inability to 'take' rather than what they normally do which is constantly and compulsively to 'give'.

### Technique
This soothing technique helps draw out deep-seated stress from the heart, shoulders, arms and hands. The massage can be finished off by gently supporting the wrist and pulling each finger in turn. Then, with the palm uppermost, massage in outward-circling movements with your thumbs. When both arms and hands have been massaged, tuck them under the towel. The hands should rest on the navel, one on top of the other (not laced) and with the tips of the thumbs touching. This soothing position is most comforting to

your partner as they feel connected to their original source of life. Prepare for the massage (Steps 1–13, page 40–42).

**Handclasp:** Take the back of your partner's right hand in the palm of your cupped left hand. Then gently clasp around the thumb joint (mound of Venus) with your left hand, creating a right palm to right palm handclasp. This comforting enfoldment is a soothing introduction to the massage.

**Step 1** EFFLEURAGE
Below. Slide your partner's hand up your forearm and effleurage (smooth) up the whole of the outside of the arm to the shoulder and down. Repeat three to six times then bend arm to massage elbow.

palm with your thumbs. Hold their hand in the starting handclasp position for a full minute before repeating on the other hand and arm.

**General Note:** Remember not to lose contact with your partner, especially after massaging the first hand and arm. Simply 'track' your fingers around their body to the other side. At the end of the treatment, cover your partner with a blanket and gently tuck them in. Leave them to rest peacefully while you bring a glass of water (slice of orange optional).

**Step 2** JOINT RELEASE
Above. Hold your partner's right hand with your right hand and ease out shoulder and elbow joint by pulling gently towards your body. Ease and release six times. Repeat Step 1 three times.

**Step 3** CONTRACTION
Above right. Hold your partner's right hand with your left hand, interlacing fingers. Support the elbow with the right hand and gently contract the hand into the shoulder to stretch the elbow. Contract and release six times, gently massaging over the elbow with the palm of the right hand to support the contraction technique.

**Step 4** FLEXING/CIRCLING
Right. With your left hand still joined to your partner's right, gently, and very slowly, circle the hand twice in a clockwise then anti-clockwise direction. Slowly flex the wrist forward and backwards twice.

**Step 5** FIGURE-OF-EIGHT
Not illustrated. Turn your partner's palm over and support it in your hands. Make a 'figure-of-eight' with your thumbs, two or three times. Finish by pressing the centre of their

Helps relieve these physical conditions: colitis, constipation, flatulence, indigestion. Helps relieve these emotional/mental conditions: anger, deep depression, addiction, anorexia nervosa, loss of appetite, bereavement, loneliness, insecurity, emotional upset, grief, shock.

### HEALING AFFIRMATION
It will help you to hold the following image and phrase in your mind during the session (optional): *There is a healing light shining in the centre of my being.*

Self-massage is often underrated, yet it is considered by many medical practitioners to be a key preventative treatment. Be gentle with yourself at all times and don't feel guilty about taking 'time out' to attend to your own needs.

### Technique
The circular technique has a fascinating effect on the body, mind and emotions. If performed in a clockwise direction it works on correcting the functioning of the internal organs. Performed anti-clockwise, it helps balance the emotional centre and greatly relieves deep depression, loneliness and addiction.

Oil your hands, wrists and forearms with carrier oil(s). Warm your hands (by chafing vigorously) and pour a little blended oil into your cupped palm. Rub palms gently together and smooth onto the body.

**Step 1** Left. Start by lying on your back with a pillow under your head and two stacked under your knees. Cross your wrists and cup your hands around your neck. If you are performing this massage for correcting the internal organs your left hand is underneath and in full contact with the torso. If performing this massage for anti-depression (anti-clockwise) then the left hand is uppermost. Draw your hands down between your breasts.

**Step 2** Right. With tips of thumbs touching, draw the left thumb down and to the side, following the line of the ribs. Make sure you apply even pressure.

**Step 3** Far right. With firm pressure, push up against the side of the waist with the left palm, gliding the edge of that hand around the pelvic bone.

**Step 4** Right. Push your hands across the lower part of the abdomen to the waist on the opposite side. Support the working hand with the right hand which is uppermost.

**Step 5** Far right. Gather in the right side of the waist with the fingers and palm of the left hand and pull back under the line of the lowest right rib, turning your fingers to point upwards. Glide your hands up between the breasts and cross the forearms.

**Step 6** Return to the starting position (Step 1) with the wrists crossed and hands cupped around the neck.

Repeat this sequence for as long as you find it comfortable and helpful.

> **General Note:** Keep your breathing as relaxed as possible and your movements continuous.

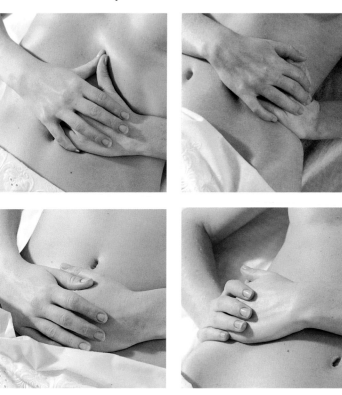

Helps relieve these physical conditions: neck and shoulder tension, headaches, otitis (ear infection), hay fever, allergies, sinusitis, colds, influenza, laryngitis, high and low blood pressure, bronchitis, catarrh. Helps relieve these emotional/mental conditions: mental exhaustion, anxiety, depression, fear, anger, lack of concentration, insomnia, disturbing dreams and nightmares.

### Healing Affirmation

It will help your partner to hold the following image and phrase in their mind during the session (optional): *My mind is ever new, open and receptive to give and receive loving energy.*

The inner strength and calming peace that the flowing movements bring enable those who are usually uncomfortable about being touched to be strengthened and regulated. In addition, by receiving regular treatment, there will be a renewed sense of mental, physical and emotional balance guaranteed to bring about a whole new positive outlook on life. These unique patterns of touch enable you to communicate without words. This is not all that unusual for we often let those around us know we care or believe in their special worth by hugging or touching them. However, this strengthening and regulating massage can transcend the act of 'hugging', bringing to it a totally different dimension.

Most people drift into a state of euphoria while receiving a massage. It is similar to the feeling we experience just before we drift off to sleep. Mentally, you are straddling the fine line between wakeful awareness and deep relaxation. As the masseur, you will soon become aware when your partner achieves this state. You can then fine-tune the communication through your own experience and heightened awareness of what is required. This intimate process transcends any sexual feelings, yet enables you to communicate with a deep sense of compassion and understanding. Essentially, massage techniques are very simple. They should help make you feel a more complete person and much more in touch with the healing energies of nature. Your hands have the power to transmit this experience to other people.

### Technique

All facial massage should be performed using upward movements. All these massage techniques are performed with the masseur standing behind their partner's head.

**General Note:** Be very careful not to massage oils around the orbits of the eyes or allow oil to enter the eye itself. In case of accident, immediately bathe your partner's eye with a weak saline solution or appropriate proprietary product. If discomfort persists, seek medical attention at the earliest opportunity.

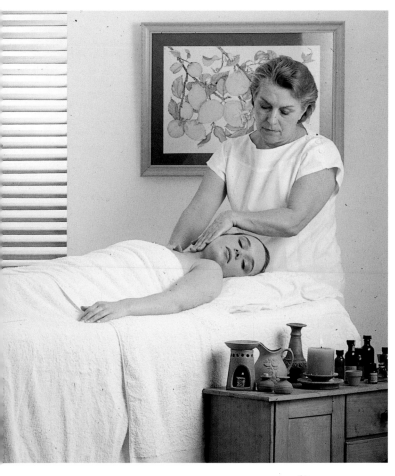

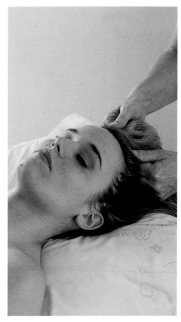

**Step 1** SCALP-DRAINING
Above. Run your fingers through your partner's hair, drawing your thumbs gently down the centre line of the scalp as far as possible. Then, moving gradually to left and right, repeat the movements until you cover the rest of the scalp. This first technique is best done without the use of oils.
Prepare for the massage (Steps 1–13, pages 40–42).

**Step 2** BROW-DRAINING
With the fingers on either side of the head, run the thumbs from the centre of the brow out to the sides until they meet your other fingers. This smoothing technique should be performed with an even pressure. Repeat six times.

**Step 3** ROCKING
Place your hands, fingers interlaced, under your partner's chin. Pull backwards and upwards towards the temples, returning to the chin in a rocking movement. At the end of the sixth stroke, gently press the thumbs into the drainage points (sited between cheekbones and nostrils) and hold there for a few seconds.

**Step 4** SWIMMING
With a smooth, breaststroke-type swimming movement, cover the surface of the upper chest. Repeat three times. Make fists, and with circular movements knuckle your fingers over the surface of the chest. Repeat three times. Then repeat the swimming movement three times.

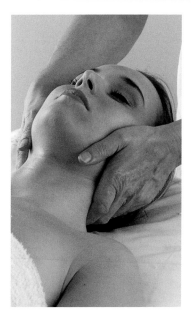

**Step 5** PIANO-WALKING
Place your hands under the nape of your partner's neck and repeatedly 'piano walk' the fingertips up and down the muscles either side of the vertebrae between the base of the skull and the base of the neck. Repeat three times.

**Step 6** ENERGY RELEASE
Cup your hands, fingers over fingers, under the back of the head, the pads of the thumbs supporting the base of the skull. Pull the head slowly yet firmly towards you to extend the back of the neck. Hold for a moment, then let the movement continue as your hands and fingers draw the hair upwards towards the crown. Pull all the way through the hair. Repeat three times.

Helps relieve these physical conditions: dermatitis, psoriasis, eczema, acne, rheumatism, cellulite, oedema, overweight, underweight, cystitis, candida/thrush, flatulence, hay fever, allergies, sinusitis, catarrh, headaches, constipation, indigestion. Helps relieve these emotional/mental conditions: addiction and alcoholism, smoking, eating disorders, imbalance of energies, nervous tension, depression, anxiety, fear, anger, grief, loneliness.

### HEALING AFFIRMATION

It will help your partner to hold the following image and phrase in their mind during the session (optional): *In relaxing, I am healing* or, *I am free to grow.*

Most people find the thought of performing the complete body massage a little daunting, so in order to add further clarification, I have combined some of the various techniques you have previously learned into an easy step-by-step sequence. I am sure this will prove most enjoyable once you have practised a few times. Be patient and all the movements will start to form a pattern under your hands.

### Technique

The reference chart on the right is designed to help you locate the various reflex areas on the feet. Prepare for the massage (Steps 1–13, pages 40–42). Spend ten minutes on the treatment as an overture to the main massage sequence. Look up from time to time

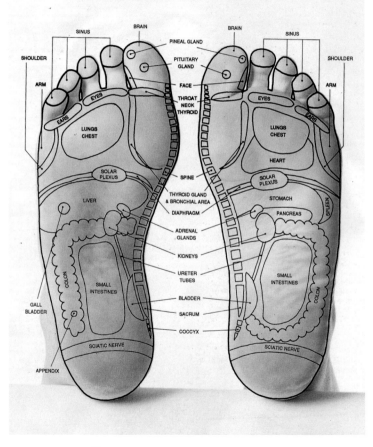

to see if your partner has any sensitive spots which may well indicate blockages. This is an outline of the practice which you may find helpful. Since so many of today's diseases are stress-related, a reflexology treatment from a qualified practitioner can be of enormous benefit for a wide range of ailments.

The points on the chart correspond to each organ, gland and structure in the body. Energy flows through channels or 'meridians' that end in reflex points on the hands and feet. When the energy flow is unimpeded, you enjoy good health. When blocked by tension or congestion, disease and imbalance occur. By applying gentle pressure to the area marked on the chart, with either thumbs or a rounded quartz crystal, the blockages are broken down and cleansed tension released and harmony restored.

The treatment chart is not so much a guide to treating a specific ailment (although there is nothing to prevent you pinpointing any areas of discomfort which are an indication of certain weaknesses in the body) but a complementary supplement to a full body massage. Reflexology is an excellent meter of your general health and a useful way of discovering which parts of the body

**Caution:** Do not practise on pregnant women.

need special treatment during the aromatherapy massage treatment.

Work down the foot from the area which relates to the head to the areas which relate to the other parts of the body.

**Step 1** INTRODUCTION TO FOOT REFLEXOLOGY
Try to maintain eye contact with your partner whenever possible so that you can immediately detect any signs of sensitivity in their feet. Place your partner's feet at the same level as your lap, or even slightly higher, and use talcum powder if you do not intend to continue on to a full body massage. Oils and creams are not as a rule used in reflexology.

Wrap your left hand (below) around the toes of your partner's right foot (holding them straight), and work your right thumb by walking it forward along the reflex by successively bending and unbending the thumb joint a little. Be careful not to bend it too much and dig your nail in. Work through the reflexes from head to toe on both feet in turn, using this caterpillar-like motion.
**Finishing Touch:** Sandwich each foot in turn between your hands and pull the foot through with a smoothing motion. Wrap the feet in a warmed towel when treatment is at an end.
Reflex Points: An easy way to remember the reflex points is to imagine a picture of the whole body superim-

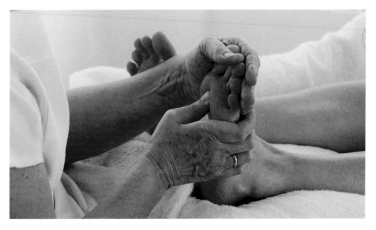

posed on the soles of the feet.

**Technique:** Press and slightly rotate your thumb(s) on each spot for three seconds to disperse any 'granules' (blockages) from underneath the surface of the skin.

**Duration:** Ten minutes as a preparation for aromatherapy; 45 minutes for the complete reflexology treatment.

**Step 2** Not illustrated. BACK (UPSIDE-DOWN FIR TREE)
Stand or kneel at your partner's head. Press fingers down either side of the spine at the base of the skull and smooth along the muscles towards the lower back (as far as you can comfortably reach). Open hands out and draw palms in and up the sides of the body towards the armpits. Repeat three times. Move to the left side of your partner, maintaining contact with your right hand.

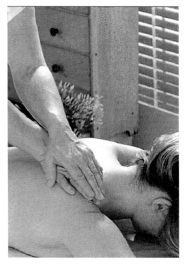

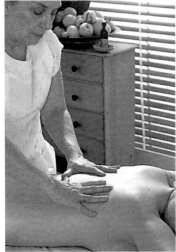

**Step 3** SHOULDERS: FIGURE-OF-EIGHT
Above. With one hand on top of the other, give firm effleurage in figure-of-eight movements around right, then left, shoulder blades. Repeat six times. Slide hands down to the base of the spine.

**Step 4** BACK (FIR TREE)
Above right. Place hands on the lower back either side of the spine to form a 'fir tree'. Push up the spine and out across the shoulders. Gently brush down the sides to the starting position. Repeat three times. Trail the hands up to the neck.

**Step 5** NECK-KNEADING
Opposite above. Knead the muscles either side of the neck between thumbs and fingers to ease out tension and any knots which have formed. Repeat Step 4, Fir Tree, three times. Cover the body with a towel and tuck it in then trail the hands down to the feet.

**Step 6** FEET: PIANO TWO
Opposite below. Walk the fingers over the soles of the feet from toes to heels. Repeat three times. Slowly lower the leg and repeat three times on the other foot.

**Step 7** LEG-SMOOTHING
Below. Stand to one side of your partner. Place your hands over the ankle and lower calf of one leg and smooth up the centre of the calf and thigh.

When you near the buttocks, open your hands to either side of the thigh and brush down the sides to the starting position. Repeat three times on both legs.

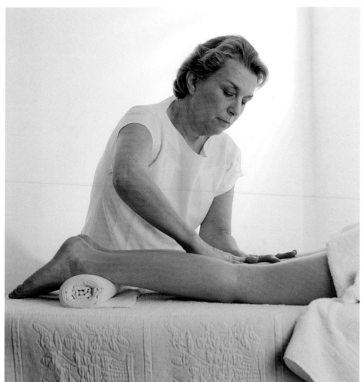

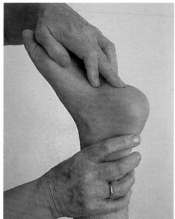

**Step 8** LEG EFFLEURAGE

Right. Place your left hand on the left ankle. Smooth upwards towards the buttock and slide down to the outer thigh. As the left hand starts to descend the leg, the right hand brushes upwards to just above the knee. The left hand crosses over the top of the right to touch the ankle ready to start again. Repeat three times on both legs. Help your partner to turn over and repeat the massage on the front of the legs. Cover your partner with a towel and tuck it in. Trail your hands up to the head.

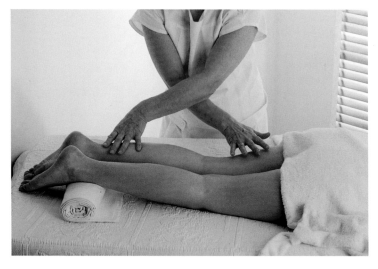

**Step 9** SCALP-DRAINING

Below left. Run your fingers through your partner's hair, drawing your thumbs gently as far as possible down the centre line of the scalp. Then, moving gradually to left and right, repeat the movements until you cover the rest of the scalp.

**Step 10** BROW-DRAINING

Far right. With the fingers on either side of the head, run the thumbs from the centre of the brow out to the sides until they meet your other fingers. Repeat three times.

Please remember to perform the Waterfall technique before and after the massage (page 42). Your healing thought: *I autograph my work with excellence.*

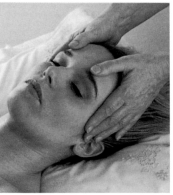

**Step 11** NECK:  PIANO-WALKING
Below. Place your hands under the
nape of your partner's neck and
repeatedly 'piano walk' the fingertips
up and down the muscles either side
of the vertebrae between the base of
the skull and the bottom of the neck.

**Step 12** CHEST: 'SWIMMING'
Right. With a smooth, breaststroke-
type swimming movement, cover the
upper chest. Repeat three times. Make
fists, and with circular movements
knuckle the fingers over the surface of
the chest. Repeat three times, then
repeat the swimming stroke three
times.

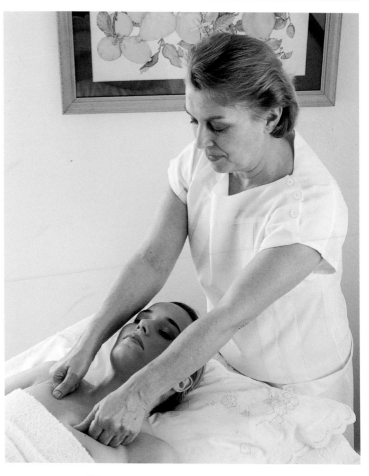

**Step 13** ABDOMINAL SELF-MASSAGE
Below. Perform the self-massage technique (see pages 56–57), but on your partner. Standing at your partner's left side, cross your forearms and place your hands on opposite shoulders. Draw the hands together (one on top of the other) and glide down between the breasts. Draw the edge of the hands down to the side of the waist along the line of the lowest rib. Then push the hands up around the pelvic bone, across the lower part of the abdomen to the waist on the opposite side. Pull back under the line of the lowest rib and turn your fingers to point upwards. Glide up between the breasts and cross the forearms to resume the starting position. Repeat three times. Cover the body with a towel.

**Step 14** HANDS AND ARMS
Below. Hold your partner's right hand with your left hand, interlacing fingers. Support the elbow with the right hand and gently contract the hand into the shoulder to stretch the elbow. Contract and release three times, gently massaging over the elbow with the palm of the right hand to smooth the

contraction technique. Hold their hand in a handclasp (see page 55) for a minute before repeating on the other hand and arm. At the end of the treatment, cover your partner with a blanket and gently tuck them in. Leave them to rest peacefully while you bring a glass of water (slice of orange optional).

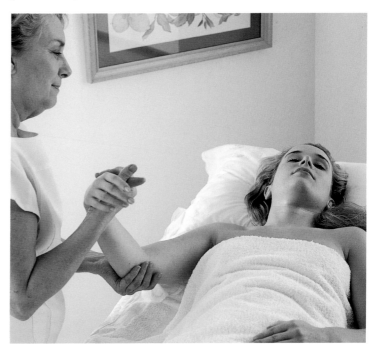

## ACNE

Bergamot, cedarwood, geranium, juniper, lavender, neroli, patchouli, peppermint, rosemary, sandalwood, tea tree.

*Too much sebum produced by the sebaceous glands. Bactericidal and anti-depressant oils are particularly valuable. CBM, FM, B, CC, SL.*

## AGEING/MATURE SKIN

Frankincense, geranium*, jasmine, neroli, lavender, patchouli, rose, sandalwood*.

*Dry, discoloured, sagging skin. Massage face and scalp to stimulate blood circulation and healthy new cell growth. Use vigorous scalp massage – gentle on the face. CBM, SM, B, CR, SL.*

## ALLERGY/SENSITIVE SKIN

Bergamot, camomile*, clary sage, jasmine, lavender, melissa, neroli, patchouli, sandalwood, ylang ylang.

*Bacteria, viruses or pollutants may cause an over-reaction of the body's defence mechanisms (hay fever, eczema, nettle rash, some types of asthma). Decrease stress levels. CBM, B, CC, SL.*

## ANOREXIA NERVOSA

Bergamot*, camomile, clary sage, jasmine, lavender, neroli, rose*, ylang ylang.

*Inability to eat coupled with psychological disturbances. Best treatment should include psychotherapy, change of diet, encouraging social eating and seeking to change attitudes to food and sexuality. CBM, B, SL.*

## ANXIETY/TENSION/STRESS

Basil, benzoin, bergamot, camomile, cedarwood, clary sage, frankincense, jasmine, lavender, marjoram, melissa, neroli, orange, patchouli, petitgrain, rose, sage, sandalwood, thyme, ylang ylang.

*Abnormal anxiety, tension and stress may express themselves in a wide range of physical symptoms. The causes are many and varied and really must be tackled at root level. Aromatherapy treatments can, however, help significantly. CBM, B, VP, NI.*

## ARTHRITIS

Benzoin, camomile, cedarwood, fennel, juniper, lavender, lemon, marjoram, pine, rosemary.

*Inefficient elimination of uric acid due to imbalanced body chemistry; often the result of stress and anxiety. Very painful inflammation of the joints, whether rheumatoid or osteoarthritis. Stress Management and Yoga are the best long-term solutions. LM, B, HC.*

## ASTHMA

Bergamot, camomile, cedarwood, clary sage, eucalyptus, frankincense, jasmine, lavender, marjoram, melissa, neroli, rose, rosemary.

*Muscle spasms cause difficulty breathing out through reduced airflow. A build-up of mucus can lead to bacterial infection and bronchitis. Attacks triggered by stress, allergens, cold air or infection. Practice Yoga and other stress-reducing techniques and check diet and nutrition. NI, VP, LM.*

## BLOOD PRESSURE
### (High)

Clary sage, hyssop, lavender*, marjoram, melissa, ylang ylang*

*Strain is imposed on the heart by continued raised blood pressure. Can lead to kidney damage, stroke or coronary thrombosis. Changes in diet and lifestyle required. CBM, B, VP, MDR.*

## BLOOD PRESSURE
### (Low)

Cinnamon, hyssop, lemon, peppermint*, rosemary*, sage, thyme.

*Sufferers prone to fainting and dizziness, feel cold and tire easily. Use vigorous massage, particularly on the feet to improve circulation. CBM, B, NI.*

## BRONCHITIS (Acute)

Basil, bay, benzoin, bergamot, cedarwood, eucalyptus*, frankincense, hyssop, lavender, lemon, marjoram*, myrrh, pine, rosemary, sandalwood, tea tree*, thyme.

*Inflammation of the bronchial tubes, fever with a painful cough. Usually originates from a viral infection. Keep patient warm and avoid irritants such as smoke and dry air. B, LM (chest/throat), SI, VP.*

## BRUISES

Fennel, hyssop, lavender*, lemon, marjoram, rosemary, sage.

*Increase local circulation to disperse bruising. When bruise discolours use rosemary. B, CC.*

## BURNS

Camomile, lavender*, tea tree.

*Apply lavender neat to minor burns. It is antiseptic and analgesic. Helps reduce pain, promotes rapid healing and reduces scarring. Treat major burns with neat oil on sterile gauze replacing periodically. B, GD.*

## CANDIDA/THRUSH

Geranium, lavender, lemon, myrrh, sage, tea tree*.

*When this yeast organism proliferates outside the gut as a vaginal infection it can lead to nausea, headaches, depression and abnormal fatigue. Use tea tree in low dilution or as a low proportion of the blend. B, D.*

## CATARRH

Camomile, cedarwood, eucalyptus, frankincense, hyssop, lavender*, myrrh, peppermint, pine, rosemary, sandalwood, tea tree*, thyme.

*Production of excess mucus due to inflammation of the mucus membranes that line the respiratory passages. Often follows infections such as colds and flu or may be due to irritants such as pollen or dust. Try excluding wheat and dairy products from the diet. SI, FM (2% dilution), VP.*

## CELLULITE

Black pepper, fennel*, geranium, juniper, lavender, rosemary.

*Not strictly a medical condition but rather a state of accumulated fat usually affecting women. Deposits of fibrous collagen collect on the outer thighs, hips and buttocks. Check the body's toxicity and for a sluggish lymphatic system. Fennel tea daily. LM, B, T.*

## CIRCULATION (Poor/Sluggish)

Benzoin, black pepper*, cinnamon, juniper, lavender*, lemon, marjoram, pine, rose, sage.

*When the body's flow of blood is restricted, a range of ailments can occur including angina, chilblains, cramp, dizziness, frostbite, and varicose veins. CBM, B.*

## COLD SORES

Bergamot*, eucalyptus, tea tree.

*Blisters which occur when overtired or run down or when suffering from an infection such as a cold. NA (1–2 drops).*

## COLDS

Basil, bay, benzoin, cinnamon, eucalyptus*, frankincense, hyssop, lavender*, lemon, marjoram, melissa, myrrh, peppermint, pine, rosemary, tea tree*, thyme.

*A viral infection of the upper respiratory tract. Inflamed mucous membranes are vulnerable to bacterial attack leading to sinusitis, bronchitis and ear infections. SI, B, NB (Lavender), LM (Chest/Neck), VP.*

## COLIC

Cinnamon, clary sage, fennel, juniper, lavender, patchouli, peppermint.

*Spasmodic stomach pains (in babies most often caused by milk in feeding); in growing children and adolescents often caused by fear of a coming event or ordeal; in adults abdominal pain can be caused by contraction of the bile duct or intestine when trying to pass poisoned food or gall-stones. B, LM (abdomen-clockwise), T (fennel).*

### COLITIS

Camomile, fennel, lemon-grass, rosemary.

*Chronic inflammation of the large bowel which becomes ulcerated, leading to pain in the abdomen and intermittent bouts of blood-stained diarrhoea. B, LM (abdomen-clockwise).*

### CONSTIPATION

Black pepper, fennel*, marjoram, orange, rose, rosemary*, ylang ylang.

*Often the result of stress, anxiety or shock. Suppressed emotional problems can cause retention of waste products in the digestive system. Change diet to high fibre as a first precaution. CBM, LM (abdomen-clockwise), T (Fennel), B.*

### COUGHS

Benzoin, eucalyptus, frankincense, hyssop, juniper, lavender, marjoram, melissa, sandalwood, thyme.

*Reflex action of the air passages provoked by inflammation of the throat's mucus membrane. SI, LM (throat/chest), HC, VP (night).*

### CRACKED/CHAPPED SKIN

Benzoin*, camomile, lavender*, myrrh, patchouli, rose, sandalwood.
*Cracked skin due to exposure to water, detergents etc. If infection is present, use benzoin neat or make up as a cream or lotion. B, CC, SL, LM.*

### CUTS/WOUNDS

Benzoin, bergamot, camomile, eucalyptus, geranium, hyssop, juniper, lavender*, lemon, myrrh*, rosemary, tea tree*, thyme.

*Most oils are antiseptic and analgesic but should only be used on minor lesions or as an emergency treatment until stitches or medical treatment can be obtained. NA, GD.*

### CYSTITIS

Bergamot*, camomile, cedarwood, eucalyptus, frankincense, juniper*, lavender*, pine, sandalwood, tea tree'.

*Inflammation of the bladder, usually caused by bacterial infection, which is both a common and occasional problem primarily in women. D (Bergamot 1 per cent dilution), HC, LM (gently over lower abdomen), B, NI.*

### DEPRESSION

Bergamot*, camomile, clary sage, cinnamon, geranium, lavender, melissa, myrrh, neroli, orange, peppermint, petitgrain, rose, rosemary, sandalwood, ylang ylang.

*The choice of antidepressant oil(s) varies according to the type of depression; fatigued and lethargic or restless and irritable. CBM, B, VP, NI.*

### DIARRHOEA

Benzoin, black pepper, camomile*, cinnamon, eucalyptus*, fennel, lavender, melissa, myrrh, neroli, orange, peppermint, petitgrain, rosemary.

*Caused by a too rapid passage of food through the intestines, preventing water from being absorbed into the system. Inflammation of the intestines occurs due to bacteria, viruses, drugs, poisons and allergy most ommon physical causes; stress, shock, fear and anxiety the common emotional/mental causes. Give plenty of water to prevent dehydration. B, HC, LM.*

### EMOTIONAL EXHAUSTION

Basil, benzoin, camomile*, clary sage, jasmine*, juniper, lavender, marjoram, rosemary.

*These are people who you would describe as 'living on their nerves'. This is nervous exhaustion with a consequent physical and emotional imbalance leading to periodic breakdown. CBM, B, VP, NI.*

### FLATULENCE

Bergamot*, black pepper, camomile*, clary sage, fennel, hyssop, juniper, lavender, marjoram, myrrh, peppermint, rosemary.

*Usually follows a meal containing gas-producing foods. If persistent, consider dietary changes. If after a course of antibiotics, take live yoghurt or lactobacillus tablets. B, HC, LM (abdomen-clockwise).*

**FLUID RETENTION** Camomile, eucalyptus, geranium, juniper*, patchouli, rosemary, sage, sandalwood.

*Excess fluid (oedema) in the tissues, premenstrual fluid retention or puffiness in legs and ankles from long standing. Failure to expel toxic wastes requires a detoxification programme to be truly effective. LM, B.*

**GRIEF & BEREAVEMENT**
Benzoin, camomile, lavender, marjoram*, melissa, myrrh, rose

*Nothing but time and healing will allay grief. However, regular aromatherapy treatment can help enormously, if only for the healing and loving touch. CBM, B, VP, NI.*

**HEADACHE**
Basil, lavender, lemon-grass, marjoram, melissa, peppermint, rose, rosemary.

*May be caused by congestion, mental effort, poor posture, fatigue, eyestrain, stuffy rooms etc. Always check the obvious: posture, diet and pollutants. If symptoms persist seek medical advice. NA (on temples), CC (temples/forehead/back of neck), SI, VP.*

**INDIGESTION**
Basil, camomile*, fennel*, lavender, marjoram, peppermint*.

*Discomfort in upper abdomen or chest, often accompanied by belching when acid is sometimes brought up into the mouth. CC or LM (stomach), T (camomile, fennel, peppermint), B.*

**INFLUENZA**
Bay, benzoin, bergamot, cinnamon, eucalyptus*, lavender*, lemon, peppermint, tea tree*.

*A term used to describe various viral infections. Treat at the very first sign. HB (3–4 drops), SI, VP.*

**INSOMNIA**
Bay, benzoin, bergamot, camomile, clary sage, juniper, lavender, marjoram, neroli, orange, petitgrain, sandalwood, thyme, ylang ylang.

*A symptom of the stress-filled modern lifestyle. Any of the sedative oils will be helpful. Check diet, posture, stimulating drinks and chemical additives. CBM, B, VP, NI.*

**KIDNEYS**
Camomile*, eucalyptus, cedarwood*, fennel, frankincense, geranium, juniper*, lavender, lemon, pine, rosemary, sage, sandalwood, thyme.

*Essential oils have a powerful effect on the kidneys because they circulate in the bloodstream and pass through the kidneys many times a day. Diuretic oils increase the flow of urine and expel toxic waste. Tonic action can be found in camomile, cedarwood and juniper. MDR, B, HC, LM (gentle).*

**LEUCORRHOEA**
Bergamot*, lavender, myrrh.

*Vaginal discharge – may be a symptom of infection or irritation. Seek medical treatment if this condition persists. MDR, D (1 per cent essential oils in boiled water cooled to blood heat).*

**LOSS OF APPETITE**
Bergamot, black pepper, camomile, hyssop, juniper, thyme.

*Can have a huge range of causes, mostly emotional/psychological, sometimes due to convalescence. B, CBM, VP.*

**MENOPAUSE**
Basil, bergamot, camomile*, clary sage, geranium*, hyssop, jasmine, juniper, lavender*, melissa, neroli, rose, rosemary, sandalwood, ylang ylang, thyme.

*The transitional period when menstruation ceases can manifest itself in problems such as very heavy periods, hot flushes, dizzinesss and fainting, depression and insomnia. CBM, B, NI, VP.*

**MIGRAINE**
Basil, clary sage, eucalyptus, lavender, marjoram, melissa, peppermint.

*Severe headache, seemingly due to restricted blood supply to the brain. Often associated with stress and trigger foods such as cheese, chocolate, red wine. Also check for bad lighting or industrial and household chemicals. CC (forehead/temples), HC (back of neck), LM (neck/shoulders), VP.*

## MUSCLES (Lack of Tone)

Black pepper, lavender*, lemon-grass, marjoram, neroli, peppermint, rosemary.

*For a tonic effect use baths and massage regularly in combination with gentle regular exercise and stretching. Yoga would be ideal. CBM, LM, B.*

## MUSCLE SPASM

Bergamot, black pepper, camomile, clary sage*, fennel, juniper, lavender, marjoram, melissa, neroli, peppermint, rosemary, sandalwood, thyme.

*The antispasmodic oils can relax the smooth muscles of the internal organs; indigestion, diarrhoea, colic etc. LM, HC, B.*

## MUSCULAR ACHES/PAINS

Bergamot, black pepper, camomile*, cinnamon, eucalyptus, lavender*, marjoram*, neroli, pine, rosemary*, sage.

*The analgesic (pain-killing) effect of the oils listed are essential muscle toners which can be applied prior to all strenuous sports and training and are a relaxing tonic afterwards. CBM, LM, B.*

## NAUSEA/VOMITING

Basil, black pepper, camomile, cinnamon, eucalyptus, fennel, lavender, lemon, melissa, peppermint, rose, sandalwood.

*Nausea and vomiting can have a variety of physical causes or be a symptom of emotional upset. B, WC (stomach area), T (Camomile, Fennel, Peppermint).*

## PERIODS (Painful)

Camomile*, clary sage, jasmine, juniper*, lavender*, marjoram*, melissa, peppermint, rosemary*, sage.

*Period pain or menstrual cramps are caused by spasms or contractions of the uterine muscles. LM (very gently over abdomen), HC, B.*

## PERIODS (Scanty)

Basil, clary sage*, fennel, juniper, lavender, myrrh*, rosemary, sage.

*The oils will bring on or increase scanty menstruation. Women whose flow is normal or heavy should avoid the oils above. CBM, B, NI, VP.*

## PREMENSTRUAL TENSION

Bergamot, camomile*, clary sage*,

geranium, lavender, melissa, neroli, rose, rosemary*.

*Physical symptoms may include fluid retention, tender breasts, swollen abdomen, nausea, headaches, anxiety, stress, anger and depression. Use lymphatic drainage massage, diet and Yoga. CBM, B, NI, VP.*

## PSORIASIS

Bergamot*, camomile, juniper, lavender.

*Skin becomes reddened, thickened, taking on a scaly appearance because the dead cells are shed slower than the new growth. Stress is usually an underlying factor and aromatherapy can certainly help in this regard. Moistened oatmeal scrubs can exfoliate the skin, but in the long term rely on reducing stress, changing diet and vitamin and mineral supplements. B, CC, ST.*

## RHEUMATISM/GOUT

Bay, camomile*, cedarwood, eucalyptus, juniper, lavender*, lemon, marjoram*, pine, rosemary*, thyme.

*Rheumatism tends to express itself either as arthritis or gout in the joints or as rheumatism and fibrositis in the muscles. Local massage will stimulate local circulation and remove toxins. B, HC, LM.*

### SHINGLES (Herpes Zoster)
Bergamot*, eucalyptus, tea tree.

*Caused by the same virus as chicken pox and produces a painful rash in a band around the torso. Often triggered by stress or when physically run-down. NA, NB.*

### SHOCK/PANIC/HYSTERIA
Camomile*, clary sage, marjoram, melissa, lavender*, neroli*, peppermint*, petitgrain, rosemary, ylang ylang.

*Neat inhalation from the bottle (like smelling salts) or a few drops on a handkerchief. Hysteria (violent outbreaks of emotion) is sometimes a response to shock. Dr. Bach's Rescue Remedy is the sovereign treatment. CBM, B, VP, NI.*

### SINUSITIS
Bay, eucalyptus, lavender, peppermint, pine, rosemary, tea tree*, thyme.

*Narrow sinuses get blocked and infected when mucous membranes become inflamed due to cold, hay fever, catarrh. Can lead to severe headaches and even meningitis if not dealt with in time. Check sensitivity/allergic reaction to wheat and dairy products. SI (6 times/day), FM.*

### SORE THROAT
Benzoin, lavender, lemon, lemon-grass, myrrh, pine, sandalwood, thyme.

*Due to bacterial infection or irritation due to coughing. SI, LM, G.*

### STOMACH ULCER
Bergamot, camomile, geranium, lemon, rose.

*Thought to be caused by bacteria but is aggravated by excess acid. Most heal without treatment.*

### URINARY TRACT INFECTIONS
Bergamot*, camomile, eucalyptus*, fennel, frankincense, geranium, juniper*, lavender, sandalwood, tea tree*, thyme.

*Women are generally more susceptible to bladder infections, e.g. cystitis, due to bacterial infection. MDR, B, HC (lower abdomen & kidney area), LM (gentle).*

### VARICOSE VEINS
Juniper, lavender, lemon, peppermint, neroli, rosemary.

*Loss of elasticity in the vein walls – a symptom of a generally poor circulatory system. Leads to aching and fatigued legs. Caused by prolonged standing, poor nutrition, obesity or pregnancy. Massage only above the varicose area. B, CC.*

| KEY TO A–Z OF TREATMENT | |
|---|---|
| **CBM**=Complete Body Massage | |
| **LM**=Local Massage/Rub | |
| **FM**=Facial Massage | **SM**=Scalp Massage |
| **NA**=Neat Application | **CR**=Cream |
| **SL**=Skin Lotion | **BS**=Body Scrub |
| **B**=Bath | **HB**=Hot Bath |
| **NB**=Night-time Baths | **SI**=Steam Inhalation |
| **NI**=Neat Oil Inhalation | **G**=Gargle |
| **CC**=Cold Compress | **HC**=Hot Compress |
| **WC**=Warm Compress | **GD**=Gauze Dressing |
| **D**=Douche | **T**=Tea/Tisane |
| **MDR**=Medical Diagnosis Required | |
| **ST**=Skin Test | **VP**=Vaporizer |
| *=Most widely recommended | |

# CHAPTER TWO
# MASSAGE

## INTRODUCTION

*M*y interest and experimentation with massage stems from years of adjusting and correcting my students' posture in dance and yoga classes.

*Exercise is one of the key ways of achieving a type of self-massage. Sound exercise can stretch, strengthen, stimulate and soothe deep-seated muscles from inside out. It also helps us to get in touch with ourselves and develop a deeper awareness of our bodies and the different stress areas that need help.*

*Caring touch is a natural instinct that can be developed through massage. The beneficial results never cease to amaze and impress me. There was, for example, the student with five demanding children who started out with very low self-esteem. The outcome of her interest in massage was that she lost nearly two stones in weight and gained confidence in the process because she taught her children to reciprocate the massage she so lovingly gave them. I believe that, even more importantly, she got to the root of her own problem, which was learning how to balance the giving and taking of energy within herself.*

*The old adage, 'a hug a day keeps the doctor at bay', is a very appropriate sentiment as far as massage is concerned. Caring for others through the power of touch is a way of showing your concern and a way of bringing sympathy and comfort to the care-worn and sick. Massage offers just such an opportunity and can be one of the most rewarding aspects of living.*

*By a process of observing myself and others, I have learnt to touch without self-consciousness and to give from the heart to guide others along the path to more positive health. It has been a slow process, learning through my everyday interactions with others to develop techniques by recognizing areas of need in people's lives.*

*Massage is one of the main healing arts. It is a beautiful aspect of lovemaking, and babies and children thrive and feel comforted and secure when honestly and openly exposed to the power of compassionate touch. Massage makes the elderly feel wanted and comforted, especially when confronted with the loneliness of bereavement.*

*Opening our hearts to the healing power of massage is one of the key ways to enjoy giving as well as asking and receiving. The loving energy released helps to balance our mental, physical and emotional states and to draw out negative energies.*

*Essentially, a good massage can touch on the root causes of many everyday ailments and help to alleviate them. It is a complementary therapy that can soothe and relax, making the recipient feel and look better within a short space of time. I have written this book in an easy step-by-step way, starting with the preparatory technique of caring for the whole body. Massage does not need to be complicated. The thought of throwing your partner on a massage bed and working a few oils into the skin is certainly not the approach that will give lasting results.*

*What I am offering here is a detailed look at the preparatory stages. The practice of massage can be enhanced by incorporating the use of natural body care products. You can have great fun making up your own formulas. Start by using my own basic recipes.*

*My own students especially enjoy the initial preparation, even more so when they realize that everything they subsequently learn stems from this first important discipline. Your partner will particularly appreciate the fact that you have taken time to enhance the atmosphere and tailor the best possible treatment to their own special needs.*

Once the preparatory stages have been learnt you can proceed to other levels of healing, utilizing the therapeutic properties of plants (Aromatherapy). This can be further enhanced by knowledge and understanding of the healing systems of China and India, in particular, in the form of meridians (energy channels) and chakras (energy centres).

This, in turn, can be taken further through re-education of the mind with positive affirmations, deep relaxation and meditation. All of these methods offer a greater perception of the complex nature of illness and disease and are the only long-term answer to treatment of the human body as a whole.

There is nothing complicated about massage and I trust you will enjoy this easy step-by-step approach to these fundamental ideas and methods. I hope they will inspire you to experiment yourself and gain the maximum enjoyment from this fascinating subject.

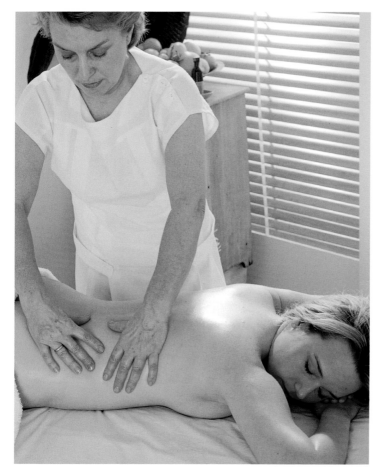

Massage can be traced back thousands of years and is probably one of the oldest therapies known to mankind. The pyramids at Sakka'ra, Egypt, were once a centre of healing in the ancient world and their walls bear depictions of people engaged in reflexology, massage and Shiatsu-like techniques.

The Greeks and Romans were known for their intense interest in the care of the body. Hippocrates, the 'father of medicine' wrote as early as the fifth century: 'The way to health is to have a scented bath and an oiled massage each day'. This sentiment is echoed today in our desire to tend, bathe and pamper the body which has resulted in steady advances and refinements in the techniques of massage and touch.

The African experimentation with hair plaiting is a form of massage and is still popular all over the world today. Pulling the hair is an excellent way of relieving pressure headaches.

Swedish massage was invented by a man called Henrick Ling at the beginning of the 19th century. He combined his knowledge of gymnastics and physiotherapy with a study of Chinese, Egyptian, Greek and Roman techniques. His basic principles of combining therapeutic massage and muscle and joint exercise are still practised today.

The next real step came in the 1970s when the American, George

Downing, laid down the basis for therapeutic massage. He considered the whole person, taking into account their physical, mental and emotional states, incorporating ideas from the Orient which included Shiatsu and reflexology.

One of the oldest and best-loved of natural therapies, massage has an enormous range of applications. The important thing to remember is that it is not a substitute for conventional medicine. Its main appeal and rightful place lies in its therapeutic value. The danger arises when we, the practitioners, feel we can actually cure people without real training when, in fact, it takes many years to perfect the technique. Once mastered, the help we can offer to others is almost unlimited.

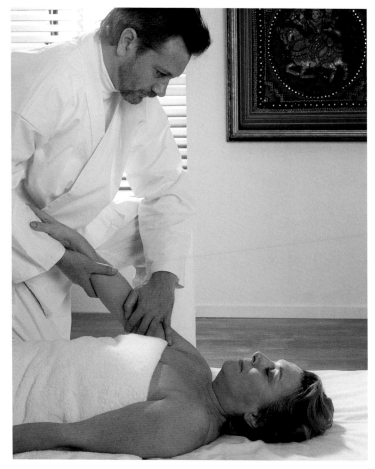

Massage is a healing art that transcends the need for words. It takes you into a different world where time itself seems to stand still. It can make you feel a different person in tune with nature and your own true self.

Here are some of the main benefits to be derived from a good massage.

**Backache:** We retain a lot of our past experiences in the form of backache. By rhythmically massaging the back muscles, particularly either side of the spine, toxins and deep-seated tensions from the past can be released and relieved. Simply resting in the 'Now' enables your partner to release the pain accumulated from the past.

**Circulation:** Is greatly improved and energy is channelled to give a feeling of deep release and relaxation which heightens awareness and body power.

**Constipation:** This can be cured with regular, remedial massage and my Wash Off Weight Formula Diet. In a nutshell, this regime includes drinking a glass of hot water first thing in the morning and last thing at night. Eat regular meals of porridge with ripe bananas for breakfast; fresh fish, new potatoes with their skins and green salads for lunch, and wholemeal cake and herbal teas at tea time. For supper, have pasta, rice or cereal with

vegetables; salad dressings should be made with pure olive oil and fresh herbs. Instead of dessert, fresh tropical fruits should be eaten first, before the meal.

**Flatulence:** The shaking and hacking movements in massage increase the vibrations that soothe the nerves of the alimentary tract which in turn relieves flatulence.

**Fluid Retention:** The lymphatic system is stimulated and is encouraged to disperse excess fluids.

**Heart:** The blood supply is increased threefold by the action of massage on the muscles and the consequent increase in the flow of nutrition to the muscle fibres and bones.

**Indigestion:** It is not a good idea to apply massage to your partner if they have eaten within the last two hours. However, massage is an excellent preventative of this complaint as it helps teach you to pace yourself and avoid rushing your food which would otherwise cause this problem.

**Muscles:** Are kept in tone and functional power increased, giving you greater elasticity and flexibility.

**Nerves:** The slow, rhythmical manipulation can produce sleep, by soothing the nerve endings.

**Posture:** Massage highlights and alerts you to your weak areas. You will soon realize that the areas causing you the most discomfort are the ones that have been neglected and misused through poor posture. Taking time out to enjoy a massage gives you the ideal opportunity to reflect on how you are using and abusing your body.

**Lack of Energy:** Massage is a great restorative, a natural tonic for your glands and inner organs, and is especially beneficial for the production and distribution of the vital lymph flow.

**Stress/Tension:** It is so easy to become obsessed with the stress and strain of everyday life and regular treatment can help to channel these feelings, releasing tension from tight, tense muscles and stiff joints. It is possible to feel the benefits for up to a week afterwards. There is nothing finer than a little pampering and the loving attention derived from a treatment.

**Headaches:** You may sometimes find that you have a headache at the end of a treatment. This is because the stress rises. Avoid this by pulling the hair during a massage when I find that tensions are released which would otherwise cause the headache.

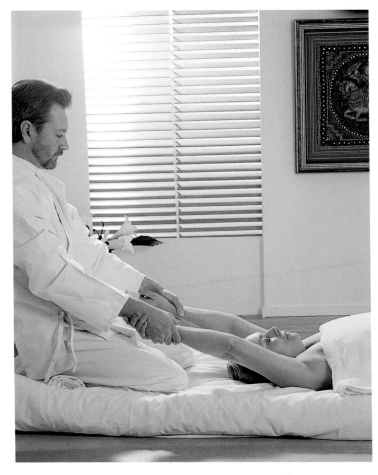

**Skin:** The tone and texture definitely improves. This is because the dead cells are exfoliated from the surface, allowing the skin to more easily absorb the natural oils being massaged, making the skin more pliable and giving it a healthy glow.

**Weight Problems:** Cellulite is the bane of most women's lives. Regular massage with essential oils, accompanied by my Wash Off Weight Formula, will work wonders. Body weight is brought into balance because the body energies are harmonized and waste products eliminated through the gentle manipulation of the whole body during a massage treatment.

**Emotions:** Deep-seated emotions such as anger, fear, frustration etc., can be released through remedial massage. It is important to allow your partner to cry should they feel the need.

Aromatherapy massage has become increasingly popular over the last few years and there are courses running in most night schools. One of the reasons for its rise in popularity is that it has the added bonus of being a truly holistic treatment. It encompasses the whole individual, mind, body, emotion and spirit, treating the human organism in its entirety.

Before commencing treatment, a complete assessment of lifestyle, including eating habits and personal relationships, should to be taken into account. It is necessary to make a thorough study of the numerous therapeutic qualities of essential oils, for it is these oils, when blended with carrier/base oils, which will make up the 'treatment' to be tailored to your partner's individual needs.

Essential oils are derived from natural sources such as seeds, flowers, fruit, peel, leaves, grass, roots, wood, bark and resins.

The primary purpose of carrier oils is as a means of lubrication for use in general massage or as a means of diluting essential oils. The reason for the dilution is that essential oils are far too concentrated in their original form and could cause irritation if applied directly to the skin.

Almost any pure vegetable oil such as soya, sunflower, or safflower can be used. These can be obtained from most supermarkets or health-food stores. Sesame seed oil is probably one of the the most suitable as it can be easily washed out of sheets and towels. Here is an outline of the most popular carrier oils:

**Rich and nourishing:**
Peach and apricot kernel, avocado: these are excellent for dry and ageing skin.

**Healing:** Olive oil for extra dry skin, e.g. psoriasis. Wheatgerm oil (rich in vitamin E) is an anti-scarring agent and needs to be blended with lighter oils, such as almond, on a 25 to 75 per cent ratio.

**Light:** Grapeseed, grapefruit or orange. These are excellent light oils which can be used on most skins.

**AVOID:** Mineral or baby oils. They are unsuitable for this purpose and clog up the surface of the skin.

## BLENDING ESSENTIAL AND CARRIER OILS

In general terms, you would expect to dilute your chosen essential oil(s) in a 3% solution with your carrier oil. This amounts to 3 drops of essential oil(s) to 5ml of carrier oil. Either use a glass dispensing jug purchased from a chemist or a 5ml medicine-dispensing spoon. For calculating quantities suitable for your partner, see section on estimating quantities below.

**Important Note:** It must be remembered that a blend of essential oils and its carrier oil is primarily a 'treatment'. The method of delivery, i.e. massage, is strictly the secondary consideration. Dosage can be quite crucial when dealing with a number of medical conditions and when your partner is vulnerable, sensitive, or in a distressed state.

## BUYING, STORING & PREPARING OILS

1. Buy the best possible organic oils from a reputable company for the very best results. Cheap oils are a false economy. Look for 'Pure Essential Oil' on the label, not 'Essence'.

2. Check they are environmentally friendly, non-animal tested and produced solely from plants and their by-products.

3. Certificates of purity are available on request. A reputable company will guarantee pure and economical products, e.g. Neal's Yard of Covent Garden, London.

4. Don't be taken in by fancy packaging.

5. If you find all your oils are the same colour then they are not pure oils. They should also vary in price from one to another.

6. Smell essential oils by testing on a handkerchief. If the smell evaporates quickly it is not a pure essential oil. Cultivate your natural intuition and senses to help you buy the best. Train your sense of smell and touch.

7. Don't be afraid to question your retailer and to ask for written information on the products.

8. Test oils for texture. If it is too viscous, leaving an oily residue on the skin, then it has had a vegetable oil added.

STORING:

1. Keep tightly sealed to prevent evaporation and deterioration through oxidation.

2. Store in a cool dark place out of direct sunlight and at an even temperature.

3. Plastic bottles will only keep oils in good conditions for up to eight weeks. Use dark brown or blue glass bottles.

4. Keep out of the reach of children and animals. Most of these oils are highly toxic if ingested.

5. Most oils, except sandalwood, cedarwood, vetiver, patchouli and rose otto can be stored in a fridge.

6. Most essential oils have a shelf life of about two years if kept in their pure state, i.e. unblended. They go cloudy as they become stale. Citrus oils have a six-month shelf life, so buy in smaller quantities. Bergamot lasts well, neroli for up to one year, whereas patchouli and myrrh actually improve with age.

WHAT YOU NEED

1. A small glass measuring/dispensing jug (from chemists) or 5ml medicine-dispensing spoon for accurately measuring carrier oils.

2. A glass eye-dropper to dispense essential oils.

3. A glass container or glazed ceramic bowl for mixing (optional).

4. Wooden or ceramic implement (miniature spatula, spoon etc.) for stirring/blending (optional).

5. Dark-tinted glass bottles for storage.

6. Self-adhesive labels and permanent (oilproof) marker/pen for labelling formulas and partner identification.

ESTIMATING QUANTITIES

A standard 5ml medicine-dispensing spoon (freely available) holds exactly 100 drops of oil. Most essential oils are used in a 3% solution. This means three drops of essential oil should be added to a 5ml spoonful of chosen carrier oil(s). Obviously one spoonful is not enough for an average adult massage, so I recommend the following proportions:

a) Baby (up to 6 months old, average size)
= 1 drop of essential oil to 5ml of a light carrier oil.

b) Child (up to 8 years old, average size)
= 2 drops of essential oil to 10ml.

c) Child (from 8–14 years old, average size
= 3 drops of essential oil to 10ml.

d) Adult (small)
= 6 drops of essential oil to 10ml.

e) Adult (medium)
= 7–8 drops of essential oil to 15ml.

f) Adult (large)
= 9–10 drops of essential oil to 20ml.

PREPARING A MASSAGE OIL

Step 1. Check contra-indications guidelines (see pages 96–97).

Step 2. Choose appropriate:
a) Carrier oil(s).
b) Essential oil formula (page 85).
c) Quantity (see above).

Step 3. Wash and rinse your hands in clean running water, scrub nails thoroughly and dry on a clean towel.

Step 4. Working on a clean, stain-resistant surface, measure required quantity of carrier oil(s) into the dispensing jar or 5ml medicine spoon. Using either the built-in dropper, or your own eye-dropper, add prescribed number of drops of essential oil(s). Check smell and test texture of oils before using in case they have combined with oxygen and turned rancid, hardened, or lost freshness. Mix with wooden spatula.

Step 5. Decant into a clean dark-tinted bottle and shake gently to blend.

Step 6. Pour into a warmed, glazed ceramic bowl, clam shell or similar and warm your hands in preparation.

Apart from base or carrier oils, which we have already discussed, there are other preparations which are useful aids to massage when for one reason or another an alternative is indicated.

### PREPARING A MASSAGE LOTION FOR FACE OR BODY
For those people who prefer the feel of a lotion rather than a vegetable-based oil, or are allergic or sensitive to certain products, a hypo-allergenic, non-perfumed, lanolin-free lotion can be used as a base.

### TALCUM POWDERS
Any talcum powder can be used (usually on the feet or hands) for reflexology-type treatments. Plain baby powder is a great favourite of mine, but there are lots of different herbal talcum powders available, such as rosemary, sage, lavender, etc. Special fungicidal powders for problem feet, i.e. athlete's foot, can be used instead of standard talcum powders. Either sprinkle the powder onto your hands, rub them together, and smooth onto the skin or, alternatively, sprinkle directly onto the feet or hands.

### BODY SCRUBS
These are excellent preliminaries or alternatives to the more traditional aromatherapy massage. They can be mixed with or without essential oils. My home recipes (page 100) work-

wonders on the skin and have the added bonus of improving the whole circulation. They remove all the dead cells leaving the skin wonderfully smooth and silky.

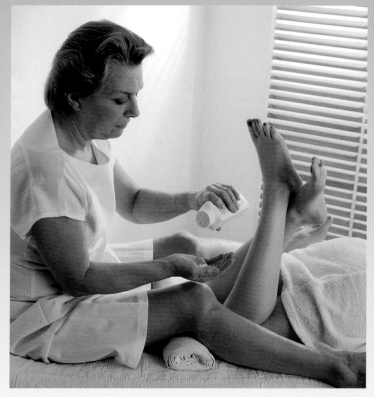

There are so many essential oils available on the market that it can be a little confusing when you first start investigating the many possibilities. (Chapter 1 (Aromatherapy) goes into more precise details.)

I suggest that you buy oils with a smell which appeals to you and then, as you start to use them and to study the numerous benefits to be derived from each one, it will be much easier to be more discerning about the oils you purchase in future. These are a few of my favourite blends:

### RELAXING FORMULA

| Body size:<br>(Essential Oil) | small<br>(drops) | medium<br>(drops) | large<br>(drops) |
|---|---|---|---|
| Jasmine | 2 | 3 | 3 |
| Orange | 2 | 2 | 3 |
| Petitgrain | 2 | 3 | 4 |
| Carrier Oil: | 10ml | 15ml | 20ml |
| (Sweet almond and/or sunflower) | | | |

**Alternatives:** Clary sage, frankincense, neroli, sandalwood, ylang ylang.

### SOOTHING AND COMFORTING FORMULA

| Body size:<br>(Essential Oil) | small<br>(drops) | medium<br>(drops) | large<br>(drops) |
|---|---|---|---|
| Lavender | 3 | 4 | 4 |
| Camomile | 3 | 4 | 4 |
| Carrier Oil: | 10ml | 15ml | 20ml |
| (Sesame) | | | |

**Alternatives:** Benzoin, bergamot, frankincense, marjoram, melissa, rose.

### REVITALIZING, UPLIFTING, STIMULATING FORMULA

| Body size:<br>(Essential Oil) | small<br>(drops) | medium<br>(drops) | large<br>(drops) |
|---|---|---|---|
| Basil | 2 | 3 | 3 |
| Marjoram | 2 | 2 | 3 |
| Juniper or rosemary | 2 | 3 | 4 |
| Carrier Oil: | 10ml | 15ml | 20ml |
| (Peach and/or apricot kernel) | | | |

**Alternatives:** Benzoin, bergamot, black pepper, cinnamon, eucalyptus, fennel, lemon-grass, marjoram, melissa, neroli, orange, patchouli, peppermint, pine, sage, thyme.

### CLEANSING AND DETOXIFYING FORMULA

| Body size:<br>(Essential Oil) | small<br>(drops) | medium<br>(drops) | large<br>(drops) |
|---|---|---|---|
| Juniper | 2 | 3 | 3 |
| Fennel | 2 | 2 | 3 |
| Lavender | 2 | 3 | 4 |
| Carrier Oil: | 10ml | 15ml | 20ml |
| (Hazelnut and/or grapeseed) | | | |

**Alternatives:** Eucalyptus, hyssop, juniper, lemon, lemon-grass, myrrh, orange, peppermint, pine, rose, tea tree, thyme.

### STRENGTHENING AND REGULATING FORMULA

| Body size:<br>(Essential Oil) | small<br>(drops) | medium<br>(drops) | large<br>(drops) |
|---|---|---|---|
| Geranium | 2 | 3 | 3 |
| Lavender | 2 | 2 | 3 |
| Sandalwood | 2 | 3 | 4 |
| Carrier Oil: | 10ml | 15ml | 20ml |
| (Sweet almond) | | | |

**Alternatives:** Bay, cedarwood, hyssop, rose, rosemary, tea tree, thyme, ylang ylang.

### APHRODISIAC FORMULA

| Body size:<br>(Essential Oil) | small<br>(drops) | medium<br>(drops) | large<br>(drops) |
|---|---|---|---|
| Clary sage | 2 | 3 | 3 |
| Rose | 2 | 2 | 3 |
| Sandalwood | 2 | 3 | 4 |
| Carrier Oil: | 10ml | 15ml | 20ml |
| (Sweet almond and/or sunflower) | | | |

**Alternatives:** Basil, cinnamon, jasmine, neroli, patchouli, ylang ylang.

---

**Pregnancy – Cautionary Notes**

It is important, during the first 3–4 months of pregnancy, to avoid the following oils: basil, cedarwood, clary sage, fennel, hyssop, jasmine, juniper, marjoram, myrrh, peppermint, rose, rosemary, sage and thyme. If you wish to use one of the suggested formulas which contains one of these oils, then replace with one of the acceptable alternatives, i.e. aphrodisiac formula, replacing both clary sage and rose with neroli and ylang ylang.

---

## PREPARING THE ENVIRONMENT

**Table/Mat:** Use either a purpose-built massage table (or light mattress/duvet if working on the floor). Position them so that there is easy access on all four sides, making sure the light does not fall directly on your partner's face.

**Interruptions:** Make sure there are no interruptions or distractions during the session together. Switch off the phone or put on your answering machine. Allow at least an hour and a half for a full body treatment.

**Music:** It is not necessary to use music. I much prefer to work in silence to the sound of the massage strokes. They can be quite as soothing and relaxing as the sound of waves on the seashore. If you do use music, make sure it is to your partner's taste. There are numerous tapes available containing natural sounds and with natural themes such as waterfalls, dolphins, birdsong, etc.

**Temperature:** Make sure the room temperature is about 70° F (21° C), slightly warmer if working on the floor. Make sure there are no unnecessary draughts and that the room has some form of ventilation: err on the warmer rather than the cooler side unless the weather is very warm when you could use an electric fan to keep the room cool and the air circulating.

**Lighting:** Artificial lighting should be subdued and indirect and natural light should be filtered, if possible. Lighted candles add a great deal to the atmosphere, even in daylight conditions. Note: Certain oils are flammable and care needs to be taken in this regard.

**Room Freshener:** As a preparation, you can enhance the effectiveness of your treatment by burning complementary oils as a welcome gesture. Sprinkle the bed/table with the leaves of freshly picked herbs or flowers (optional). Check first that the scent you choose is to your partner's liking.

**Bed Linen:** Use only natural fabrics for sheets and blankets, etc.

**You will need:** Three large bath towels in pale colours or two large cotton/linen bed sheets as a base and to cover your partner instead of towels; one woollen blanket for the rest period; three rolled towels/sheets to place under ankles, knees, forehead or neck, where necessary; four pillows (two behind head and under knees and ankles for reflexology treatment); four floor cushions for each side of the bed base if working on the floor, or small meditation stool; towelling robe (optional) for your partner. A finishing touch: scent bedlinen by sprinkling with a few herbs or spray with essential oil(s) or rosewater.

**Footcare:** Washing the feet before a treatment is an ideal way to introduce reflexology. You will need a jug and bowl of scented warm water (or cold in hot weather), pumice stone, pine cone, flannel, warm towel (in cold weather), talcum powder for treatment, crystals (optional).

**Essential oils/talcum powder/ lotions:** Essential oils are used in aromatherapy, but you can use pure vegetable oils for massage. Talcum powder is the best medium for reflexology. For body and facial treatments you need cleansing milk, cotton wool, bowl of warm water, bowl of cold water, string glove, face flannel, body spray of rose or orange flower water to spray on your partner after treatment in very hot weather. Note: If using a base/carrier oil, have a small bowl of oil at the top and bottom of the bed/base for easy access.

**Flowers/plants/stones/shells/ crystals:** These are the best natural items to use if you wish to enhance the massage area.

**Hot water bottle(s):** Can be used to warm towels before using on feet or as part of a massage treatment.

**Outdoors:** The best massages are always done in the shade of a tree. Need I say more?

### PREPARING YOURSELF

**Bathing:** Have a warm shower with a body scrub (loofah or mitt) using unperfumed products (or your choice of deodorant might clash with the treatment oils or even be offensive to your partner). Perform the cleansing process 'The Waterfall' (optional – see Psychic Cleansing).

**Psychic Cleansing (optional):** Whether you have a physical shower or not, it would be helpful to perform the cleansing process The Waterfall. Imagine you are standing beneath a clear-running waterfall. It washes through and over you, removing particles of negative energy or 'psychic dirt' from your 'aura' or electromagnetic body.

**Hair:** Tie back loose hair.

**Hands/Nails:** Check your nails are clean, cut very short, and polish-free. Wash your hands in warm water to remove any grit or stickiness as a gesture of respect for your partner's comfort. If you have a cut on your hand or forearm, make sure it is covered with a waterproof dressing.

**Clothing:** Wear comfortable, loose-fitting clothes in white or soothing colours. Make sure your shoes are low-heeled and comfortable or, preferably, work in bare feet.

**Skin Test:** It may be stating the obvious, but do check that you, yourself, do not have an allergic or adverse reaction to the range of oils that you propose to use in the treatment.

**Pregnancy:** If you are pregnant, check that there are no contra-indications to oils you propose to use in your partner's treatment.

**Record Book:** Keep a note of the massage techniques, treatment oils used etc., to see how you and your partner progress through successive treatments.

**Final Check:** Check through your massage techniques so that they are uppermost in your mind during the treatment (see pages 91–93).

**Refreshment:** Have a glass of water at hand in case you need a drink during the massage treatment. Remember that you, the masseur, are also receiving an aromatherapy treatment through your hands/arms. You will need to hydrate your body just as much as your partner.

### ALIGNING AND PREPARING YOUR PARTNER

**Health Enquiry:** Before you start a treatment you should make basic health enquiries of your partner (see contra-indications guidelines page 96). Discuss any stressed, damaged or painful areas in their body. Posture is a key clue, so make a point of observing any imbalances and weak areas, e.g. over-extension of knees can create all sorts of physical and mental tensions. Be alert to any indications of emotional or mental stress as these offer vital clues when it comes to selecting aromatherapy oils. If in any doubt, consult a doctor or trained aromatherapist.

**Bathing:** Offer a shower to your partner prior to treatment since the skin should be as clean as possible and free from deodorants, body lotions and cosmetics if you are using aromatherapy oils. (A body loofahed or scrubbed of dead skin would make the treatment more effective.) Offer your partner the chance to visit the bathroom before you start the treatment.

**Clothing/Jewellery:** All your partner's clothing should be removed if they are having a full body massage, except in the clearest case of extreme modesty or self-consciousness. All jewellery and rings should be removed apart from wedding bands.

**Massage Position:** Ask your partner to lie on their back on the massage bed with their head within a few inches of one end for easy access. Rest their head and knees on a pillow, using extra pillows or towel rolls as necessary. Ensure that your partner is as relaxed and comfortable as possible. Cover their legs, hips and upper torso with three warmed towels or large cotton/linen sheet (scented optional).

**Body:** Observe the manner in which your partner walks, moves and mounts the massage table or settles onto the bed/floor. This will give a good indication of any inflexible areas that would benefit from your gentle touch. Assist them to lie centrally on the bed with the head near to the end for easy access.

**Head:** Ensure that the crown of the head is in line with the base vertebrae, chin at right-angles to the chest. The head should rest on a pillow or the neck on a rolled sheet or towel. Remember to soothe away any worry lines during the massage. Lips and eyes should only be lightly closed. The tongue should not adhere to the roof of the mouth and teeth should be unclenched.

**Hair:** The hair should be back from the face and away from the back of the neck. Keep drawing the hair away from the head wherever appropriate during the massage.

**Scalp:** Once contact is made, you will be able to see, and feel, the tension areas in the scalp. A great deal of tension is, in fact, held in the scalp, so don't forget to work on it with your fingertips or use a firm hairbrush, working well into the scalp. Some people have very sensitive skin, so care should be taken as to the appropriate level of pressure. Encourage dialogue and feedback if you are unsure.

**Chest:** Ensure the chest is open and relaxed with the shoulders resting on the base of the bed or pillow(s).

**Breathing:** Ask your partner to take a few deep breaths or sighs to physically and mentally relax themselves.

**Back:** If there is any curvature or distortion, adjust the pillow support so that your partner is as comfortable as possible. Caution: Please remember not to massage over the vertebrae. Wideness at the top of the spine can indicate tension in the shoulders and wideness at the base can indicate tension in the lower back and pelvic area.

**Legs:** Make sure that the legs are relaxed and open from the hips and, if your partner is lying on their front, rest the ankles and feet on a pillow or towel roll.

**Feet:** If the toes are crooked or webbed, be careful when stretching or even stroking them. Flat insteps need a little tender loving care and your partner should be encouraged to have their posture corrected by an Alexander technician. Caution: If your partner is ticklish be very firm with your touch and, if necessary, start by massaging over their socks.

**Abdomen:** If the abdomen is very tight, your partner may well be holding in a lot of emotional tension, so gently coax the muscles with your palms, edges or back of palms. Encourage deeper breathing – the greater the exhalation, the greater the relaxation to follow.

**Arms:** Your partner may have difficulty 'giving their arms up', so shake them a little to encourage the letting-go process. Don't forget to open the arms and massage into the armpits.

**Hands:** It is always appreciated if you end with a loving hand clasp of the left hand (heart side).

**Skin:** Look for tell-tale signs on the skin i.e. extra-dry or oily areas, stress lines, cellulite, different tones or colour, varicose veins, rashes, cuts, bruises, blemishes, etc. These areas will either need to be avoided or you will need more oil and a little extra attention.

**Joints:** Be extra careful if soothing over inflamed or distorted joints.

**Choosing Your Oils:** If you are using aromatherapy essential oils, make up a customized blend (see pages 82–83).

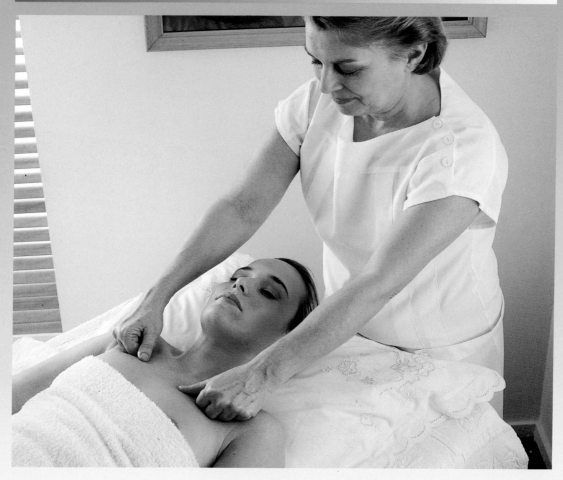

**Scent Check:** Before blending, let your partner smell and approve your selection of treatment oils. Let their intuition and preference form part of your choice of ingredients. Sometimes, a strong aversion to a particular oil can indicate that some part of the preparation is harmful to this individual. Learn to trust these signals.

**Skin Test:** Prepare your oils (page 82–83). Test the blended oil on your partner's forearm. If irritation or redness appears, change or dilute the blend. Note: A number of factors such as menstruation, stress and certain drugs may heighten sensitivity to this test.

THE MASSAGE PRACTICE

**Psychic Cleansing (optional):** 'Negative' psychic energy/psychic dirt, can build up in/on your partner's aura/electromagnetic body. If your partner is generally in a fatigued or lethargic mood then, with your hand an inch or two above the body, stroke/brush the energy up and off the body from toes to head. If your partner is very much 'in their head' and tense or nervous, stroke/brush their energies from head to toes. Periodically, shake your hands away from the bed/table to throw off the energy. Alternatively, flick the energy into a small bowl of sea salt granules. The salt can later be cleansed by standing it in sunlight.

**The First Touch:** Start your aromatherapy massage by gently touching the body through the towel to make physical contact. Some people will have more physical 'armour' than others: this is a good way of breaking down unnecessary barriers.

**Covers:** Uncover the part(s) of the body to be massaged. Remember to replace the coverings after the part(s) has been massaged to keep it warm.

**Sequence:** To gain the full benefits of massage, work on the body as a whole whenever possible, rather than a localized area. The sequence I prefer is as follows: feet (with partner lying on their back), back (with partner lying on their front), buttocks, back of legs, (turn body) front of legs, head, face, neck, chest, abdomen, arms, hands. If this does not feel right for you, experiment with other sequences until you find one that suits the way you wish to work.

**Oiling:** Oil your hands, wrists and forearms with carrier oil(s). Warm your hands by rubbing them briskly together. Pour a little oil into your cupped palm. Rub palms gently together and smooth over the area to be massaged. Replenish the oil as required.

**Aromatherapy Note:** If your partner's skin is particularly dry, absorbent or hairy and is absorbing the blended amount to such an extent that you think you may not have enough to finish the treatment, supplement with as much carrier oil(s) as you require. Remember, the 'dosage' of essential oils is a calculated treatment, so do not make up more blended oils to replenish the ones you have used.

**Contact:** Start the massage with a gentle touch and, once you have made contact with your partner, try to keep it until the entire treatment is completed.

**Awareness:** Whether you are standing, sitting or kneeling, check your posture from time to time during the massage session. If you are standing, make sure your weight is evenly distributed on both feet. Rock from one foot to the other with the longer flowing movements. Use your weight, rather than your muscles to apply pressure.

**Role Reversal:** Remember, you are massaging a person and not just skin, flesh and bones. Put yourself in their place from time to time and make sure they are aligned, comfortable and warm at all times.

**Hands/Arms:** Don't be afraid to use, and experiment with, every part of your arm – from fingertips to elbow. Massage with the fingers, knuckles, palms, backs and edges of the hands, wrists, forearms and elbows.

**Strokes:** Perform each stroke between three and six times, no more, as it may cause irritation. Each stroke should flow into the next and after the sixth a 'smoothing-off' stroke should be performed. Never drag your movements downwards. Keep the fingers together in a massage technique and slightly apart in an aromatherapy treatment. Always work your strokes towards the heart where possible.

**Flexibility:** Keep your hands and wrists flexible, moulding your hands over the contours of the body. Keep your wrists, elbows and shoulders relaxed throughout the massage.

**Breathing:** Keep your breathing natural, i.e. breathe on impulse. Don't hold your breath. This can happen when you are concentrating too hard. Breathe with the flow of the movements. Once you have become more adept you will be able to synchronize your strokes with your partner's breathing patterns. If you find they are holding their breath, encourage them to let go.

**Pressure:** Be sensitive to any changes taking place due to the pressure you are applying, and respond accordingly. Ask your partner for feedback if you are not sure what they would prefer. Pressure should never be so great as to cause pain or discomfort, although it is very much a matter of individual pref-

erence. Be sensitive to both the age and condition of your partner. Work with the muscles rather than against them. Coax them into relaxation. Certain conditions respond better to one level of pressure than another, e.g. use a greater pressure for those suffering depression and a lighter one for those suffering from high blood pressure. Your intuition will eventually be your best guide.

**Rhythm:** With the exception of percussion-type movements, i.e. 'hacking' and 'cupping', all massage should be slow, gentle and rhythmical. An even tempo is essential to encourage a sense of relaxation. There is no advantage in harsh movements since the flow of blood and lymph is comparatively slow.

**Repetition:** It is not necessary to exactly duplicate every stroke. Allow variations as your intuition dictates. In time, this will produce new techniques, ideas and refinements to your own individual style. You and your partner are the best judges of whether or not a certain technique works.

**Continuity:** Keep the flow going. Don't worry if a particular technique is missed out. The very best masseurs work intuitively with the individual needs of their partners in mind.

**Cautionary Areas:** Ease stressed muscles and joints but don't press on any

bones, vertebrae, on kneecaps or behind the knees, on swollen muscles or joints. Do not apply any massage techniques other than a very light, featherlike touch to bruises and inflamed areas. Caution: Never massage varicose veins or legs where thrombosis is present.

**Cuts & Wounds:** Apart from the obvious discomfort you would cause your partner if you massaged on or over a cut or wound, you must consider the modern-day hazards of infection. If your hands have any cuts or wounds there is always the possibility of viral contamination. They must be sealed with water/oil-proof dressings.

**Conversation:** Keep your conversation to a minimum but allow your partner to talk if they need to, especially if it is to comment on a particular technique or stroke.

**Stress Release:** Encourage your partner to feel free to release deep-seated stress with sighs or even crying. Crying is very healing. Do not be tempted to 'comfort' their distress. Without removing the sympathetic presence of your touch, simply allow them the opportunity to 'discharge' what they are feeling. Often, nothing need be said. Points raised by your partner can be discussed after the session, if appropriate. It is time well spent, even if it means you have to shorten your massage programme to accommodate this interlude.

### MASSAGE AFTERCARE

**Resting Period:** When the massage is complete, cover your partner with a warmed blanket (if necessary) and leave them to rest on their own for 10–15 minutes.

**Refreshment:** Offer water to hydrate the system (with an optional slice of orange/lemon/lime unless they suffer from arthritis).

**Aromatherapy Note:** Encourage your partner to drink more water during the next few hours. Emphasize the importance of this point.

**Cautionary Advice – Massage:**
Advise your partner of the following:
a) The possibility of drowsiness and the need to take extra care if driving or using machinery.
b) The possibility of headaches which can sometimes occur after a massage, due to the release of stress and toxins into the blood stream – it sometimes gets worse before it gets better!

**Cautionary Advice – Aromatherapy:**
Advise your partner of a) and b) above, plus the following:
c) Not to drink alcohol for up to six hours after the treatment (otherwise they might get extremely drunk).

d) To avoid heat treatments such as hairdryers, sunbeds and infra-red appliances for up to six hours after treatment.
e) Not to sunbathe on the same day as their treatment if they have had citric oil or a high proportion of bergamot in the blend of oils.
f) To allow as many hours as possible for the treatment to take effect before taking a bath or shower (preferably up to 12 hours).
g) To wear loose-fitting clothes for as long as possible to allow the skin to breathe freely and to try not to rush around after a treatment.
h) That urine may appear darker and stronger-smelling (since toxins are often released by the treatment).

**Feedback:** Encourage constructive feedback from your partner and ask them to relate any specific points of interest or concern. Massage is a very personal and often liberating experience for someone who has been rather stressed or anxious. Be prepared: your partner may wish to talk about quite personal problems. Listening is as much a part of massage as the techniques you have just employed. You would be well advised to give yourself an extra margin of time after the massage/treatment to accommodate this aspect of the session. If you have to hurry your partner away immediately after the massage it can leave them feeling 'unfinished'. This can undo

much of the good work you have done, even if that was first class!

**Reciprocation:** Massage can be an even more enjoyable experience if your partner is willing to reciprocate the massage you have given, either immediately or at a later date. This will dispel the sometimes uncomfortable 'expert/client' relationship. At the heart of a treatment is the concept of balancing the flow of energies within our own body/mind/emotions and helping those we care about to do the same. The mark of a good masseur is one who recognizes and displays these characteristics in both their human relationships and the very strokes they use as techniques.

Useful advice to help you choose appropriate oils, make a basic health assessment of your partner and observe important massage safety guidelines.

1. Blood Pressure (high): Maintain a light touch in your massage.

2. Body Conditions: If giving an aromatherapy treatment, take note of the following factors or observations to help choose the most appropriate essential oils:

   a) dietary problems (i.e. diabetes, overweight, underweight, anorexia nervosa, bulimia, ulcers, colitis, constipation, flatulence, diahorrea, indigestion)

   b) muscle tone and texture (i.e. tense, relaxed, contracted, tender, unconditioned)

   c) skin type (i.e. dry, oily, sensitive, cracked, irritated, inflamed, blotchy)

   d) circulation (i.e. sluggish, poor)

   e) spine (i.e. curvature, distortion, spondylosis)

   f) joints (i.e. stiff, inflamed, painful, inflexible, swollen)

   g) systems under stress (i.e. nervous, muscular, digestive, skeletal, circulatory, urinary, respiratory, etc.)

   h) mind and emotions (i.e. stress/tension, depression, anxiety, grief, loneliness, fear, anger, apathy, lethargy, oversensitivity, trauma, lack of concentration, shock, addiction, insecurity, confidence (lack of).

3. Epilepsy: Seizures may be controlled with such substances as ylang ylang, lavender and camomile.

4. Energy Levels: Check your partner's energy levels (i.e. overactive, busy, calm, tired, irritable, low).

5. General State of Health: Query your partner's general state of health and, if you can without prying, find reasons, i.e. physical factors such as infections, colds, flu, sinusitis, etc., problems in a relationship/family, school, work, etc.

6. Homeopathic Remedies: If your partner is taking homeopathic remedies, get them to check with their practitioner before using essential oils.

7. Hydration: It is most important to hydrate the system after an aromatherapy treatment. Please offer your partner a glass of water after treatment and encourage them to drink more water to help the process.

8. Medication: Take into account any medication being taken by your partner as it can have adverse effects when combined with aromatherapy. Consult a medical practitioner.

9. Mental and Physical Handicap: Partners with handicaps can be treated very successfully provided you reduce any aromatherapy formula to half strength at first. Increase when you feel it is safe.

10. Sleep Patterns: Find out if your partner is sleeping well, cannot sleep, is having difficulty in getting to sleep, waking early or waking unrefreshed, or is suffering from insomnia.

11. Safety:

    a) Keep essential oils out of the way of children and animals as many are toxic in their concentrated forms.

    b) Tightly screw tops on bottles after use and keep in a cool dark place out of sunlight.

    c) Wipe any spillages from working surfaces to avoid staining.

    d) Keep oils away from eyes. Note: never massage within the orbits of your partner's eyes and in case of an accident wash in a saline solution and seek medical advice if irritation persists.

    e) Remove jewellery (except wedding bands) during treatments.

    f) Only use prescribed amounts of blended oils as they are very potent. If you run out, use as much additional carrier oil as you need.

12. Time: Take up to one and a half hours for a full body massage or aromatherapy treatment and allow your partner to rest quietly on their own for 10–15 minutes ensuring they are comfortable and warm.

13. Treatment: Prepare for treatment (pages 87 et seq.) and attend to

the little details as they will be appreciated by your partner.

14. Young Children: If you are preparing an aromatherapy treatment for children up to the age of 7 years, use diluted quantities of essential oils in their bath, i.e. 1–2 drops.

Contra-indications to help you avoid mistakes when choosing essential oils. How to make a basic health assessment of your partner and observe important massage safety guidelines.

1. Acupuncture: An aromatherapy treatment should not be given if your partner has had acupuncture that day.
2. Alcohol: Do not give a massage to anyone with substantial amounts of alcohol in their system. Advise your partner not to drink alcohol for at least six hours after an aromatherapy treatment if they wish it to be effective.
3. Asthma: Do not treat advanced cases with aromatherapy.
4. Back Problems (slipped disks, damage, injury, whiplash etc.): In cases other than muscle strain, ask your partner to seek the advice of a specialist such as an osteopath, chiropractor or physiotherapist before giving a massage.
5. Baths: Do not give an aromatherapy treatment to anyone who has had a hot bath immediately prior to a session. A warm shower or bath is advised before any massage.
6. Blood Pressure (high): Do not use rosemary essential oil.
7. Cuts, Swellings, Sprains, Boils, Carbuncles, Septic Conditions: Do not massage over them.

8. Cancer: Give only gentle hand and face treatments.
9. Deodorants: Ask your partner not to use deodorants or body preparations if they are planning to have an aromatherapy treatment.
10. Driving: Advise your client not to drive or use machinery if they feel at all drowsy after their massage.
11. Eating: Do not massage your partner if they have eaten within the previous two hours or have had a drink within the last half hour.
12. Energy Levels: Do not give a massage if your energy levels are low or you have a cold or flu.
13. Epilepsy: Do not use rosemary, hyssop, sweet fennel and sage essential oils.
14. Heart Conditions: Do not treat advanced cases.
15. Heat: Advise your partner to refrain from exposing their body to the heat from hairdryers, sunbeds or saunas for at least six hours after an aromatherapy treatment.
16. Hernia: Do not massage over the affected area.
17. Inoculation: Do not give an aromatherapy treatment to anyone who has had an inoculation within the previous three weeks.
18. Internal Use: Although acceptable in the form of commercially available teas, it is generally not recommended for any one other than a trained aromatherapist to pre-

scribe herbal substances to be taken by mouth.
19. Massage Oils: Do not use mineral oils, use only pure vegetable oils.
20. Operations: Do not give an aromatherapy treatment to anyone who has had an operation within the previous six months.
21. Periods: Do not give an aromatherapy treatment to anyone dur-

ing their period. You can use sedating oils, not stimulating oils, for two days either side of the period itself.

22. Pregnancy: There are certain oils which must be avoided in the early stages (3–4 months): aniseed, armoise, arnica, basil, birch, camomile, camphor, cedarwood, clary sage, cypress, fennel, hyssop, jasmine, juniper, lavender, marjoram, myrrh, origanum, pennyroyal, peppermint, rose, rosemary, sage, savory, thyme, wintergreen, plus any other oil with toxic properties.

23. Skin Infections: Never massage infected areas.

24. Sunbathing: Advise your partner not to sunbathe on the same day as their aromatherapy treatment if you have used citric oil or a high proportion of bergamot in the blend of oils. These have tanning agents and can affect the pigmentation of the skin.

25. Swollen Limbs: Do not massage: there is a danger of breaking the skin by overstretching.

26. Thrombosis: Do not massage or treat anyone with thrombosis.

27. Varicose Veins: Only massage above the varicose area, not on it, and never below as this will only increase the pressure in the vein.

**Aromatherapy Caution:**
If you or your partner breach any of the above guidelines, the aromatherapy treatment will not only be less effective but could be dangerous in certain circumstances.

**Health Warning:**
If in ANY doubt about such items as medical conditions, PLAY IT SAFE and consult a medical practitioner or trained aromatherapist before commencing a treatment or massage. Ultimately, you must use your common sense and discretion as to what extent these guidelines may he relaxed. Last of all, GET YOURSELF TRAINED!

It is pointless having a body massage if you have neglected to prepare the skin. This special treatment is a must for those occasions when you want to look and feel your very best. Other than that, it is one of the ways of giving yourself some extra tender loving care when life seems to be moving too fast.

The treatment is much more effective if given by a friend but it is quite possible to give yourself a body scrub. This particular idea was inspired by my dear friend, Suzie Spears, a well-known aromatherapist and remedial masseur.

There are all sorts of recipes you can make up yourself from my sample recipes on page 100-101. My own particular favourite is one I made up for clients whilst working in the Caribbean. I chopped the top off a fresh coconut, scooped out the milk and flesh, mixed it with chopped nuts, oats, dried grated coconut and cocoa butter. My client's skin was like velvet after rinsing off the scrub under a sparkling waterfall – the essence of romance! I hope you have as much fun experimenting with your own ideas.

**Step 1** Right. Prepare the recipe for your own or your partner's skin type. Use approximately one third of the scrub for the back and backs of the legs, one third for the front of the torso and fronts of legs and one third for the face and arms. In addition to the body scrub you will need a basin of

warm water, a face flannel, string glove or natural bristle brush, towel (warmed), large leaves or cling film. Note: It is quite easy to contain the debris from the scrub if you give the treatment on the floor using a mattress base covered with a large cotton/linen sheet and spread wide. Shake it outside and feed the birds!

**Step 2** Below. Using half the mixture, rub it over your partner's back and upper arms using gentle friction and light pressure. This will remove much of the dead skin and allow the new skin to breathe. In addition, the stimulating action of the massage has a overall tonic effect on the circulation. Note: Psoriasis is a skin condition caused when the new skin forms faster than the dead skin is sloughed off. My Tonic Scrub recipe (page 101) should help significantly with this troublesome condition.

**Step 3** Below. Cover the scrubbed area with large fresh leaves (if available), or cling film and, over that, a warmed towel. Leave the scrubbed area for approximately ten minutes to allow the oils to really penetrate. In the meantime, use the scrub on the backs of the legs and cover. Return to the back, remove the towel, leaves/cling film and brush off the scrub with a string glove or natural bristle brush. Do the same with the backs of the legs.

Turn your partner over and repeat the scrub on the front of the torso (chest and abdomen only) and fronts of legs. Cover, and use the remaining mixture for the arms and face. Cautionary Note: Do not apply any scrub within the orbit of the eyes, on the lips or in the ears. Do not cover the face with a towel or cling film and be very gentle and careful when removing the scrub from the face with warm water. Offer your partner a warm shower or, better still, a dip in the sea if working on the beach.

This is a selection of some of my personal formulas. Have some fun experimenting and designing your own recipes.

## FRUIT AND NUT SCRUB

All-purpose scrub for normal and balanced skin types
**Ingredients:**
Wild oats (2 tablespoons),
Mixed chopped nuts (2 tablespoons),
Finely ground almonds (2 tablespoons), Grated rind of one orange,
Almond oil (4–5 tablespoons approx.)

Aromatherapy treatment (optional):
Add 3 drops each of geranium and neroli essential oils.

### Method:
Blend by hand, in a mixing bowl, all the ingredients to form a moist, pliable paste. Add more oil if necessary. Do not liquidize as the resulting mixture would then be too fine for its exfoliating, scrubbing purpose.

## CARIBBEAN SCRUB

For dry skin
**Ingredients:**
Dessicated coconut (2 tablespoons),
Mixed chopped nuts (2 tablespoons),
Finely ground nuts (2 tablespoons),
Grated rind of one lime and one lemon,
Avocado and/or coconut oil
(4–5 tablespoons approx.)

Aromatherapy treatment (optional):
Add 2 drops each of camomile, jasmine, neroli and rose essential oils since they improve general skin health and blood supply to the skin's growing layers. Alternatively, 3 drops each of geranium, lavender and sandalwood, which have a normalizing effect on the production of sebum, the skin's natural oils.

### Method:
Blend as for Fruit & Nut Scrub.

## HARVEST SCRUB

For oily, acne- and blackhead-prone skin
**Ingredients:**
Rolled oats (3 tablespoons),
Granary flour (1 tablespoon),
Dessicated coconut (2 tablespoons),
Vodka (1 tablespoon – optional),
Grated rind of one lime or one lemon, Juice of one lime or lemon,
Grapeseed and/or hazelnut oil
(4–5 tablespoons approx.)

Aromatherapy treatment (optional):
Add 2 drops each of bergamot, cedarwood, sandalwood, to control bacteria, or 2 drops each of bergamot, geranium, lavender essential oils, which have a normalizing effect on the production of sebum, the skin's natural oil.

### Method:
Blend as for Fruit & Nut Scrub. Finishing Touch: After the body scrub treatment (see pages 98–99 for technique) use ripened sliced pears for an astringent action on very oily areas.

## Oriental Scrub

For ageing or mature skin
**Ingredients:**
Parboiled brown rice (3 tablespoons),
Poppy seeds (2 tablespoons),
Wheatgerm (2 tablespoons),
Runny honey (1 teaspoon),
Half a pulped avocado,
Chopped fresh rosemary leaves
(1 teaspoon),
Avocado and/or wheatgerm oil
(4–5 tablespoons approx.)

Aromatherapy treatment (optional):
Add 3 drops each of frankincense, sandalwood to combat dullness and crêpey texture or 2 drops each of geranium, jasmine, neroli or rose essential oils which have a normalizing effect on the production of sebum.

### Method:
Blend as for Fruit & Nut Scrub. Finishing Touch: Remove scrub into a

bowl, and wash off surplus with warm water and a face flannel.

## Tonic Scrub

For dry, flaky, dehydrated, tight, psoriasis-prone skin
**Ingredients:**
Jumbo oats (2 tablespoons),
Fine oats (2 tablespoons),
Ground rice (2 tablespoons),
Sesame seeds (2 tablespoons),
Jojoba and/or olive and/or arachis (peanut) oil (4–5 tablespoons approx.)

Aromatherapy treatment (optional):
Add 2 drops each of bergamot and lavender and 1 drop each of camomile and juniper essential oils.

**Method:**
Blend as for Fruit & Nut Scrub. Finishing Touch: Once the scrub treatment is complete (see pages 98–99 for technique), soothe the psoriasis-affected area with freshly sliced cucumber and leave for 5–10 minutes.

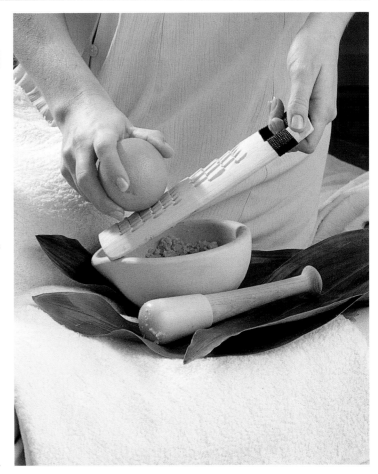

### NATURAL TREATMENTS TO ENERGIZE AND UPLIFT

On that fateful day when you stare into the mirror at a lined and haggard stranger, wondering whether you could possibly justify the cost of a face-lift, you may seriously have to consider some form of 'damage limitation'.

First the good news. It doesn't take plastic surgery to achieve youthful features, just a few basic techniques that will make you the envy of your friends.

Start with a smile – it's the finest face-lift and will not only raise your spirits but the hearts of those around you. Acknowledge those lines of experience that have given your face its special character, you've earned them! Confidence and feeling good about yourself is the first rule of beauty care. It is not narcissistic but perfectly natural to wish to look your best at all times.

Contrary to what the media would have us believe, it is interesting to find just how liberating it is to discover your own natural self. Others feel much more at ease with a person who has no need to hide behind a painted mask. My mother seems to grow younger every day. She does not buy expensive cosmetics or formulas, she just lives at peace with herself. She has never ever sunbathed, so her skin has maintained its ability to produce natural oils. Skin that is well cared for may

well be lined but it can still retain that glow of vitality that makes a woman attractive well into old age.

Premature wrinkling is caused by inner conflict. All the tension and worry you have experienced in your life may well start to show in your face. Your inner self is unfolding before your very eyes. Ultimately, only by resolving physical, emotional and mental imbalances will you notice improvement. Once you have learned to honestly confront the realities of your life, even the deepest worry lines will fade.

You will look and feel so much healthier if you undertake regular, natural treatments. Body massage and daily routines of slow rhythmical exercises such as yoga, regular deep relaxation, prayer or meditation will feed your inner self. I have found these are the most important preventative measures with which to combat the malaises of everyday life.

**Step 1** HAIR COMBING

Left. Have your partner relax on their back, knees bent or resting on a pillow, feet in line with hips, arms lying freely by their sides (or resting palms on solar plexus), palms uppermost, fingers curling naturally. Place the neck on a rolled towel covered with an oblong piece of cheesecloth.

Gently draw all the hair away from the head, running your fingers through it for 2–3 minutes.

**Aromatherapy Note (optional):**
Put 4 neat drops of essential oil in a line along the centre of the cheesecloth strip. Let your partner choose between lavender, rose, basil, melissa, lemon-grass or peppermint (all excellent for headache/stress relief) or camomile, jasmine, neroli, petitgrain or ylang ylang as a general relaxant/refresher.

**Step 2** NECK STRETCH
Take hold of the ends of the cheese-cloth and lift your partner's head as far forward, chin towards the chest, as is comfortable. Hold for a few seconds, then slowly lower the head. Repeat several times, making sure the head is really relaxed and is cradled by the cloth. If you wish your partner to relax into this position it is imperative that they trust your skill and support.

**Step 3** NECK EXTENSION
With the head resting on the bed, pull up the left side of the cheesecloth, rolling the neck as far over to the right as is comfortable for your partner. Hold for a second or two then, lifting the right side of the cheesecloth, roll the head over to the left. Repeat slowly several times so that the head rolls freely from one side to the other.

**Note:** Steps 2 & 3 can be repeated by cradling your partner's head in a pillow and then in your hands without a pillow underneath.

**Caution:** Keep the crown of the head centred on the base of the spine in all the movements.

**Step 4** HAIR KNOT
Below. This simple technique can often relieve a tension-induced headache in a few minutes. If your partner has long hair, then weave it into the folds of the cloth in this technique. If your partner has short hair, then let the cloth do all the work. Explain, in advance, what you are going to do, and why. Ask for feedback so that you do not hurt them. It does, however, need to be firmly managed for full effect.

Cross the ends of the cloth over the brow, then fold the ends around the hair, slowly twisting and squeezing the knot tighter and tighter. Ask your partner to breathe out as you turn the knot and 'pull the tension' out of the head. Hold for about 10–15 seconds. Slacken the hold and then repeat 2–3 times. Remove the cloth and smooth out hair and cloth for the next step.

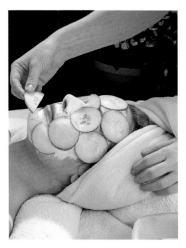

**Step 6** FACE-, CHEST- & NECK-SMOOTHING
Placing the cheesecloth strip down the right side of your partner's face (adjacent to the nose), smooth outwards to the outer edge of the face. Repeat 3–4 times on both sides. Then place the cloth across the chest and gently smooth upwards to a point under the chin. Repeat 3–4 times.

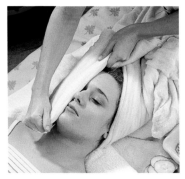

**Step 5** BROW-SMOOTHING
Using either one end of the cheesecloth or a separate piece, press down on the brow and hold for approximately ten seconds. Release the pressure and repeat 2–3 times. Very gently stroke the cloth from eyebrows to hairline, repeating 3–4 times to soothe the lines of worry away.

**Step 7** FACIAL SCRUB TREATMENT
Blend together 2 tablespoons of Fuller's Earth with one tablespoon of fine children's play sand, or finely chopped nuts, and add enough rose or orange flower water to make a smooth paste. Gently rub the mixture into the face, avoiding the orbits of the eyes, the lips and ears. Leave to set for 10 minutes. Cover with finely sliced cucumber. Leave for a further five minutes. Remove cucumber and wash off the scrub with warm water (scented with a few drops of flower water – optional) and a face flannel. Dry with a piece of cheesecloth by pressing it gently onto the face.

**Extra Special Treatment** (optional): After the facial scrub and before the massage, apply a strawberry face pack. Mix four crushed strawberries (medium size) with 2 tablespoons of fine oatmeal. Smooth over the skin (excluding eye orbits, lips and ears). Leave for 5-10 minutes. Wash off with warm water and a face flannel. Dry the skin.

**Massage:** Using evening primrose oil or Vitamin E carrier oil, massage the face from chin to brow with small circular movements of your fingertips.
**Finishing Touch:** Dip your forefinger into flower water and dab on a point just between and above the eyebrows (third eye – *tilak*).

## Natural Treatments to Enrich and Nourish

For those occasions when your hair does not seem to be your crowning glory, my olive oil treatment will give life to dry and lifeless hair. Your hair affects the way you feel and is a real give-away when you have lost interest in yourself and are lacking confidence.

I encourage my clients and students to try new hair styles, especially if they have had the some one for years and years. Doing your hair differently can give you a whole new outlook on life – I've seen it happen time and time again! It definitely changes the energy in and around your head. I would not go as far as to recommend a colour change as I think well-groomed natural hair has a softer look. Bottled potions can also make people look 'hard-edged' and the result never looks quite natural. There will also be a time when you have to face the issue of when to give up the battle against encroaching grey hair.

The way hair is cut, managed and cared for is far more important to the way you present yourself. Good grooming breeds confidence and I heartily admire the person who has decided to grow old gracefully without making concessions to dowdiness. In my book they have the key to eternal youth.

**Step 1** Applying the Olive Oil
Right. Firstly, warm approximately 250ml of pure, extra virgin, cold pressed olive oil. The very best quality is required to assure the tonic aspect of this technique. Do not heat quickly or to a very high degree lest you destroy some of the natural properties of this very special commodity. It is vital that you test the temperature of the mixture on the back of your partner's hand so that they approve and are prepared for the application.

Have your partner rest on a padded table, their head slightly tilted back, their neck resting on (and sup-

**Step 2** COMBING & SCALP MASSAGE
Below. Whether you partner's hair is long or short, run your fingers through the hair and scalp to work the oil in, massaging the oil thoroughly into the scalp and hair.

**Step 4** HOT TOWEL TREATMENT
(Not shown)
Wrap a warm towel around the head. Let your partner rest for at least 30 minutes to enable the oils to penetrate the hair and scalp. Remove the towel and wash the hair in a mildly astringent shampoo of your choice. Rinse well, towel, and allow to dry without using a hairdryer.

ported by) a rolled towel. Place a large bowl on the floor to catch the flow of oil.

Carefully, and very slowly begin by trickling then pouring the warm oil onto a point a little above and between the eyebrows. This is traditionally recognized by some cultures as the site of the third eye and is the location of the vestigial pineal gland. The oil will flow over the brow, through the hair and onto the scalp. This is a blissful experience! The uniquely enjoyable aspect of the treatment is the sense of deep relaxation that is felt as the oil cascades over the head.

**Step 3** WRINGING (LONG HAIR)
Above right. If your partner has long hair, lightly squeeze off the surplus oil by wringing out the hair with your hands.

**Note:** To help maintain healthy hair, try to avoid drying out the natural oils with hairdryers, sunbathing, chemical colourants and perming solutions. Brushing the hair and scalp regularly helps to stimulate the scalp and balance its natural functioning.

### NATURAL TREATMENTS TO CLEANSE AND DETOXIFY

The following self-help treatments will prepare you for massage and maintain the health of your body. I use these wonderful wooden bath products which are available from many health shops. They can be used either under the shower or after a bath.

Rubbing the body with a rough bath towel is an excellent way of stimulating the circulation and loosening surplus dead skin, which can have an ageing effect if not removed. I feel quite strongly that it is important to wear loose-fitting clothes, made from natural fibres, in order to maintain a healthy skin. Tight-fitting, man-made fibres restrict the proper functioning of the skin and, I am quite convinced, cause a build-up of cellulite. Nylon underwear and stockings restrict the circulation and free movement of air around the body, marring freshness and natural cleanliness.

**Step 1** DOUBLE FOOT ROLLER
Right. Place both, or either of your feet on the ridged wooden rollers. Rub the feet forward and backwards as many times as you like with a pressure that suits your level of sensitivity.

**Step 4** ARM & BODY CELLULITE SCRUB
Use a string mitt under the shower along with a special anti-cellulite soap containing pure oatmeal. Rub in small circular movements towards the heart.

**Step 2** SINGLE FOOT ROLLER
This specially curved and ridged wooden roller is particularly good for massaging tired insteps. Repeat the forward and backward movements as many times as you wish on each foot.

**Step 3** PINE CONE FOOT ROLLER
Pick a green pine cone before it has had a chance to open. Roll it over the surface of the soles of your feet, with a pressure that suits your sensitivity. Have the thicker end near the instep.

**Step 5** THIGH & BACK SCRUB
Right. This is best done under a hot or cold shower using a special anti-cellulite soap and natural bristle brush. Scrub your thighs in circular movements towards the heart, working over the whole of the thigh area on both legs. Repeat with up and down scrubbing movements over the shoulders and either side of the spine.

> **Note:** Keep hard skin from building up on the soles of the feet by regularly using a pumice stone after soaking in a warm bath.
>
> **Aromatherapy Note (optional):**
> Add 6 drops of any of the following essential oils: benzoin (max. 2 drops), camomile, lavender, myrrh, patchouli, rose or sandalwood.

To Balance and Harmonize
I decided to introduce this sequence to my massage classes to help newcomers who were rather reticent about being touched and massaged for the first time. It appeals to the basic instinct of being cradled and rocked. Most of the techniques can be adapted for one masseur, apart from Step 6, Rebirth – The Infant's Cradle, which requires 4–6 people.

As I was later to discover, the ritualistic and reverential feelings this technique evokes touches something quite beautiful and primeval within us all. There are so many ways you can explain and develop this idea; wrapping the mummy, swaddling the baby, peeling the onion, butterfly in the cocoon, etc. Both children and adults (big children) instinctively relate to the concept.

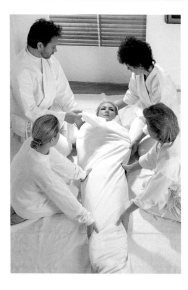

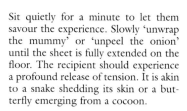

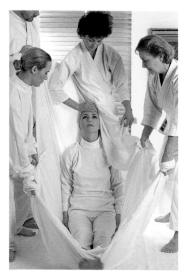

**Step 1** THE PHARAOH

Have the recipient lie on a large, strong linen sheet, with feet together. Cross their arms into the 'pharaoh position' (left hand on the right side of the upper chest, fingers touching the shoulder, right arm over the left, fingers touching the left shoulder).

Take your time as you fold one side of the sheet across the recipient's body, conforming to their outline. Fold the other side over and tuck in all round. The feet should be loosely bound in and the sides and top of the head swathed with the face uncovered.

Sit quietly for a minute to let them savour the experience. Slowly 'unwrap the mummy' or 'unpeel the onion' until the sheet is fully extended on the floor. The recipient should experience a profound release of tension. It is akin to a snake shedding its skin or a butterfly emerging from a cocoon.

**Step 2** ASCENDING THE THRONE

Unfold the arms from the pharaoh position and lay them by the side of the body. The two participants nearest the head should gather the sheet in a secure grip and lift the recipient into a partial sitting position (45°).

**Step 3** CROWNING THE BROW

Flowing on from the previous movement, the principle participant should step behind the recipient and support the back with shin and thigh. With hand cradling and crowning the brow, the body can be raised to an almost upright position. This should allow the brow to be gently stroked three times in an elevating and uplifting fashion. Use your control of the sheet to roll the back to the floor vertebra by vertebra.

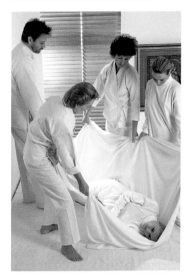

**Step 4** ROLLING
Fold the recipient's arms and place the hands lightly on the abdomen. Two participants should roll the recipient to a 45° angle with the others taking no more than a supporting role. Hold for a few seconds, then slowly roll the body to the floor. Pause, then repeat the sequence, rolling the body to the other side. Slowly roll the body to the starting position and relax the arms by the side.

**Step 5** ASCENDING TO THE GODS
Firmly clasping the feet, raise the legs very gently into a near vertical position, depending on the flexibility of the recipient's spine. Ensure that the chin is squarely on the chest and the spine is in alignment. Hold for 2–3 complete breaths before relaxing the spine, vertebra by vertebra, once more onto the floor.

**Step 6** REBIRTH – THE INFANT'S CRADLE
Adopt a secure stance with knees slightly bent, feet in line with hips and a straight, but not rigid back. Take a firm grip of the sheet and, using the power of your thigh muscles, lift until the recipient's body is well clear of the floor. Gently rock backwards and forwards like a cradle rocking in a gentle breeze. Continue for as long as is comfortable. The chief participant should watch for any signs of strain and give a sign or word to co-ordinate a controlled return to the floor.

**Step 7** THE BLESSING

Cross the recipient's arms, once again, into the pharaoh position. Rewrap the body as before and kneel close and in a near circle. In turn, place your left hands in a stack onto the recipient's solar plexus. Do not press or apply great pressure. Then, once again in sequence, place your right hands onto the stack. Close your eyes and bestow a loving blessing on the recipient and your fellow participants. One by one, slowly remove the hands. Leaving the body still wrapped for a few minutes, sit quietly and reflectively. Gently unwrap the body to complete the sequence.

**Notes:**
**a)** The sheet can be scented with essential oils, with the rejuvenating qualities of frankincense and myrrh.
**b)** There should be no communication other than a word of direction from the principle participant, although gentle background music is an option.
**c)** The whole sequence should he practised several times until the sequence is a wordless ballet of movement. This can be a training/learning experience for all the participants. It would certainly help if everyone has had the opportunity to experience being the recipient.
**d)** With four participants, have two either side of the body. With six, two either side, one at the head, one at the feet. It is as well to discuss in advance the roles you will each play. The key directing/position is at the head. It does not necessarily require greater strength, although sensitivity and good balance are prerequisites.
**e)** It is important that the recipient has complete confidence in the competence of everyone present or they will nor be able to relax, which is one of the key points of the exercise.

## Natural Treatments to Revitalize and Soothe

There are more hours lost at work due to back and shoulder problems than any other ailments. This is primarily due to unconscious misuse of the body and an innate laziness when it comes to correct body posture. Tired bodies that slump in front of the TV every night are asking for heart problems.

To be fair, there is very little guidance as to what constitutes good body posture. Standing tall is not enough: we need to learn to breathe properly and to balance our body weight evenly. Poorly taught exercise régimes, repetitive movements connected with work, badly designed furniture and cars, tightly fitting clothes, ill-fitting footwear, incorrect lifting, stress and anxiety, all contribute to general back, neck and shoulder problems.

Don't despair, for there are some excellent self-help programmes you can follow. They can radically change the quality of your health and be a preventative measure in your life rather than a remedial one!

One of the very best systems is the Alexander Technique. This identifies the habits that have become unconscious and helps you to change them for the better. It is a clear and precise approach which teaches you to use your muscles and limbs correctly in everyday movements while exercising at the same

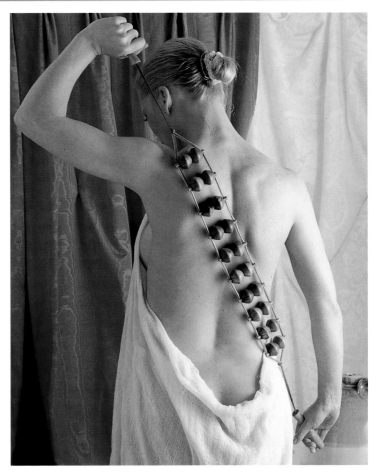

time. The overall benefit has helped many sufferers from arthritis, back pain, slipped disks, rheumatism, fibrositis and hypertension and a range of associated ailments such as sexual malfunction and mental disorders.

You need first to ease your aches and pains: so here are my steps to self-help which will have definite remedial benefits before you embark on a course of massage or consider enrolling on a course of Alexander Technique.

**Step 1** DOUBLE BACK ROLLER
Left. This roller can be used when you come out of the bath or shower. Roll over the shoulders, back and hips to release deep-seated tensions and to break up areas of cellulite around the hips and thighs.

**Step 2** BACK ROLLER
Right. This can be heaven-sent when there is no one around to massage your stiff, neglected back muscles. Either roll up and down each side of the spine from the lumbar region or over the shoulder and down and up the spine.

**Finishing Touch:** Rest with your bottom close to the wall, hips on one or two firm cushions, legs up the wall with knees bent but not restricting the calf muscles, feet in line with the hips. Rest your hands on the solar plexus and take long, slow deep breaths imagining that your pain and discomfort is flowing out with each exhalation. Allow your muscles to seemingly melt into the ground.

### TO RELEASE DEEP-SEATED AND LONG-STANDING TENSIONS

Of all the massage techniques, this is one of the most relaxing. Many of your past and present worries seem to lodge in the form of nervous tension in the back, neck and shoulder muscles.

The root cause is that you may be sitting back into your pelvis and distorting the spinal column. This puts unnecessary pressure, not only on many of the muscles, but also on the joints.

The following sequence of strokes combines 'cupping' and friction-type techniques. These help to coax the muscles into 'letting go' and relaxing long-standing tensions.

Remember to keep your massage area/room warm, otherwise, not only will you have difficulty helping the muscles relax, but your partner will not fully benefit from your efforts.

Keeping yourself warm, especially around the kidney area, is another practical way of helping yourself to a healthier spine. Your spine is only as healthy as the muscles that support it.

**Step 1** FIR TREE
Right. With your partner resting on their front (rolled towel under ankles), arms either forward or relaxed by the side, palms uppermost, start with the Fir Tree technique from the base of the spine. Place both hands on the

lower back either side of the spine, thumb and forefingers about 1½in (4cm) apart, to form a fir-tree shape. Smooth up the spine and out across the shoulders to the sides of the body,

drawing the hands down either side to the starting position. Repeat three times. As an alternative, stand at the head of your partner and reverse the procedure from neck to base.

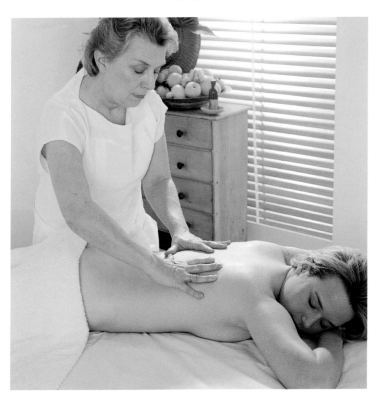

**Step 2** HACKING

The technique of hacking consists of a percussive movement that tones the skin whilst stimulating and improving the circulation. This is particularly useful for work on the back, thighs and buttocks where you seek to relieve deep-seated stress. With your hands at right angles to the body, palms facing each other, chop rapidly up and down with the edges of the hands in a rhythmical manner. Keep the fingers and wrists relaxed. If this is the first time you have tried this technique, then practise on your own body first so that you know how it feels.

Starting at the buttocks, work you way up the body towards the shoulders. Avoiding the bony shoulder blades themselves, cover one side of the back, proceeding gently across the shoulders and down the other side. Repeat this circuit three times.

**Body Note:** If you find it difficult to perform this technique on both sides of the body (standing or kneeling only on one side) then change position to the other side of the massage bed. Maintain contact during the changeover.

**Finishing Touch:** Perform Step 1, the Fir Tree once, slowly, as a smoothing-off technique.

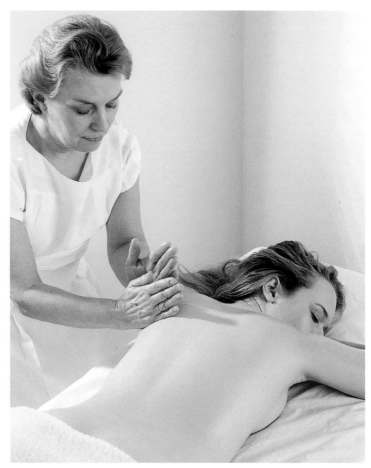

**Step 3** CUPPING
The technique of cupping is another form of percussion. Your cupped hands will trap air and produce quite a loud sucking sound. It can be performed all along the thighs, buttocks and back in a long circuit. If you are just performing a back massage, confine the actions to that area. Repeat the circuit three times.

Again, if you find it difficult to do both sides of the body from one position, then move to accommodate easy access.

**Finishing Touch:** Perform Step 1, the Fir Tree once, slowly, as a smoothing-off technique.

**Body Note:** You may well find that your partner's back needs more oil than other areas of the body.

**Aromatherapy Note:** If you are using essential oils, then supplement with base/carrier oil(s) only.

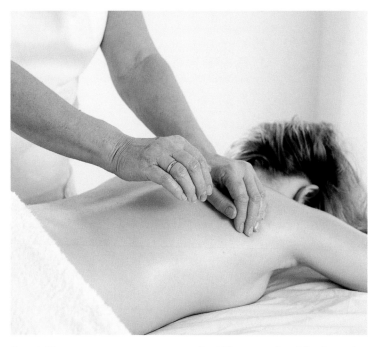

**Step 4** KNEADING
Opposite above. Beginning at the hips and working up the side of the body which is furthest from you, grasp the flesh with one hand and squeeze without pinching and push it towards the other hand. Release the first hand, then pick up and squeeze the flesh with the second hand. The action is very like kneading dough for bread. It should be a smooth and flowing action which progresses up the back to the base of the neck and over the shoulders and out across the upper arms. Change position, if required.

**Finishing Touch:** Perform Step 1, the Fir Tree once, slowly, as a smoothing-off technique.

**Body Note for Kneading:** This versatile technique can produce deep waves of relaxation if performed slowly and rhythmically. It will stimulate and invigorate if performed briskly. Kneading can be used to great effect on all the soft muscles of the legs, buttocks, back, across the back of the neck, upper chest and upper arms.

**Step 5** DRAINING

Below right. With the palms facing one another and pointing towards the head, press the edges of your hands into the muscles either side of the spine at the top of the buttocks. Press downwards and outwards (allowing the palms to flatten onto the body), drawing the muscles away from the spine and finishing with the hands either side of the body. Finish the stroke with a gentle comforting press. Bring the right, then the left hand back to the centre a few inches above the starting position and repeat the stroke. Continue all the way up to the neck until the whole of the back has been divided by this draining stroke. Work only lightly over the shoulder blades. Repeat the whole process once more.

**Finishing Touch:** Perform Step 1, the Fir Tree once, slowly, as a smoothing-off technique.

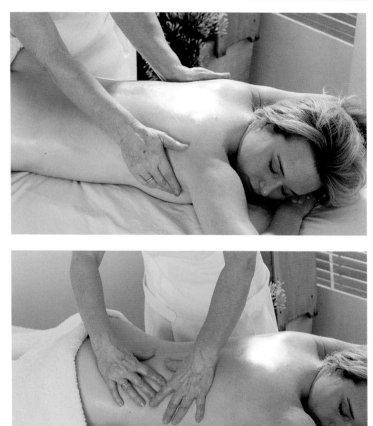

**Step 6** SHOULDER BLADE PRESS
Stand on your partner's left side and place your left over their right shoulder, cupping to support it. Form a 'V'-shape between thumb and forefinger of your right hand and place beneath the rim of the shoulder blade. As your partner breathes out, slightly raise the shoulder with your left hand and simultaneously press the thumb and edge of your hand gently under the shoulder blade. Repeat three times, moving the 'V' a little higher or deeper with each exhalation.

**Alternative:** Standing/kneeling on your partner's right side, tuck their right arm into the body, crook their elbow, and place the forearm across the back. Cup your partner's right shoulder in your right palm and support the length of the upper arm with your forearm. Use your left hand in the 'V' shape to gently press under the shoulder blade. You should practise with these two alternatives to discover what works best for you and your partner. Repeat on the left shoulder.

**Finishing Touch:** Perform Step 1, the Fir Tree once, slowly, as a smoothing-off technique.

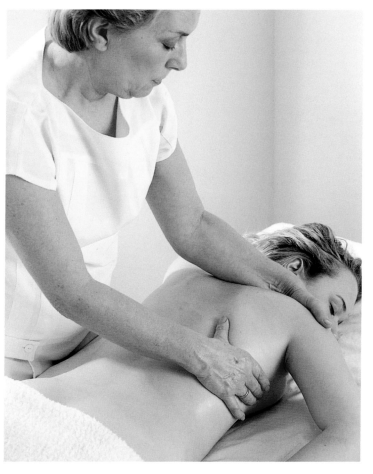

**Step 7** CRISS-CROSSING

Place you palms, side by side, on the closest shoulder near the top of the spine. Push your right palm away from you in a horizontal strip across the back. Simultaneously, as you pull your right hand back towards you, push your left hand away – they will cross halfway. Keep the criss-crossing hands moving constantly without leaving the surface of the skin, generating a warming friction as you perform this gathering/pushing technique. Once past the shoulder blades, allow your forearms to come into play as the hands extend well over the back and down the sides. Work your way down the body and up again until the whole back has been covered twice.

**Finishing Touch:** Perform Step 1, the Fir Tree once, slowly, as a smoothing-off technique.

> **Body Note:** Criss-crossing can be performed gently over the front of the body from pelvis to under the breasts.

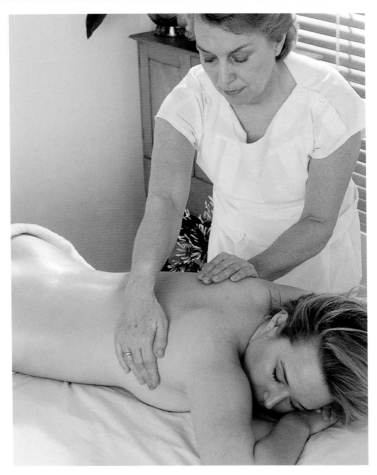

## To Soothe, Stretch and Strengthen

Shiatsu is the Japanese word for 'finger pressure', though the technique uses other body parts such as hands, feet, elbows and knees.

It is a folk medicine that dates back thousands of years. The basic principle is the belief in a vital force known as 'Ki' which flows in connected channels (meridians) throughout the entire body. Each one is linked to an organ or psychophysical function.

Any lack of Ki energy is caused through an immoderate lifestyle. Disease occurs when this Ki energy is no longer flowing freely or is more excessive in some areas than in others.

Shiatsu is an ideal self-help home practice as it simply balances the Ki factor so that your body is encouraged to heal itself.

Working with a partner, using these basic introductory steps, can give you both a valuable insight into this fascinating tradition.

Body Note: There are only two techniques used, i.e. pressure and stretching. The key to success is to be as relaxed as possible in applying the pressing and stretching. Both hands need to stay in contact with your partner's body when applying the techniques.

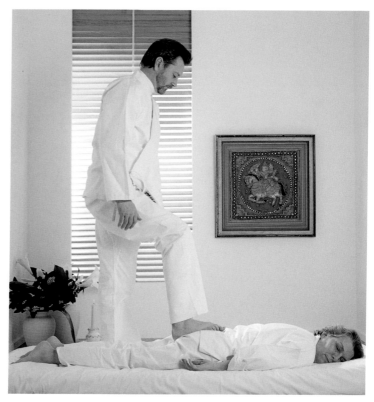

**Cautionary Note:** Anyone with back problems or a distorted spine should avoid these techniques and instead take professional advice from a trained practitioner.

**Step 1** CENTRING & SMOOTHING
Left. Have your partner rest on their front, head to one side, arms by the sides and a little away from the body, elbows slightly bent to relax the shoulders, palms uppermost, legs relaxing from hips to toes, feet in line with the hips, heels relaxed slightly outwards. The following technique will help their body relax more naturally into this position.

Stand astride your partner's legs with your feet rooted firmly on the ground, yet with a sense of lightness in all your body as it aspires towards the heavens. Let your arms hang freely by your sides. Place one foot on the lower spine between the buttocks and apply very light pressure. Gently rock your partner's body from side to side, soothing them into a state of relaxation. Repeat this motion five or six times or until you feel them 'let go' of tension or stiffness. Eventually you will sense when they let go and hand the power of movement over to you.

**Step 2** NATURAL BACK TRACTION
Right. Incorrect lifting is potentially dangerous, as far as the back is concerned. This technique teaches the importance of lifting with bent knees and using the power of the thigh muscles to do the actual lifting. There should be no strain involved when giving this natural traction to your partner.

It is vital that your partner is very relaxed before starting. Stand astride your partner's legs, bend your knees, leaning over their body to cradle the hip bones firmly in your hands. Synchronize your breathing with your partner's and on the next out-breath, lift their hips a few inches off the ground. Their knees should remain on the floor. Ensure that you have the full

dead weight in your hands. If your partner still seems a little stiff, then shift the weight slightly to left and right to encourage them to let go and give you their full weight. Hold for 3–4 complete breaths. Relax and release the position, supporting them all the time you are lowering them gently to the floor.

**Step 3** BACK-, STOMACH- & CHEST-STRENGTHENER

This technique has an all-round benefit and is excellent for people with poor posture, asthma, bronchitis, breathing problems or lack of body tone.

Sit astride your partner's legs. Bend one knee and place it in a forward position to brace against the forthcoming posture. Have your partner clasp their forearms or elbows. With both your hands, securely cup their shoulder joints. Once again, synchronize your breathing with your partner's. On inhalation, slowly pull back the shoulders until your partner's muscles offer resistance. You will have to develop sensitivity to their limitations. Hold a position that will allow both of you to breathe comfortably for 3–4 complete breaths. Slowly relax and release the posture as your partner rolls down onto the floor. Take a few breaths before repeating the sequence two or three times.

> **Body Note:** There is often a wonderful sense of revitalized energy flow associated with the release of this posture.
>
> **Note:** You must be confident in both your position and your ability to hold your partner's weight comfortably or they will not trust you enough to let go. Keep your knees bent at all times; never lock the knees.

### Natural Treatments to Refresh and Revive

Throughout the ages, foot washing has been both a practical and symbolic ceremony. It is one of the most personal interactions between host and guest in many cultures. This prelude often sets the tone for a meeting, family gathering or spiritual practice.

With this in mind, I suggest that such a practice is reciprocated and that both you and your partner share the benefits. It will be especially welcome after a long and tiring day when legs and feet are tired and aching.

This practice is often an excellent introduction for someone nervous of personal touch or massage in general. Prepare the room carefully with towel, a jug of warm, scented water, soap, foot-brush, pumice stone, nail-clippers, foot lotion and a spare bowl for used water.

**Note:** It is essential to offer a foot bath (either hot or cold, depending on the weather and the condition of the feet) before treatments such as reflexology or Shiatsu.

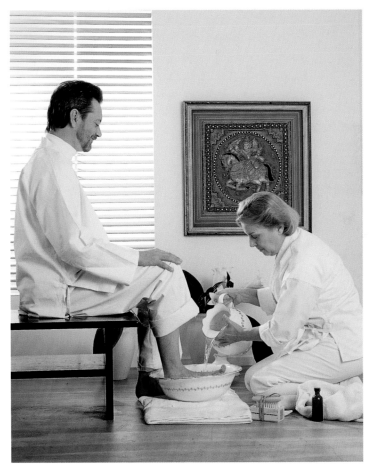

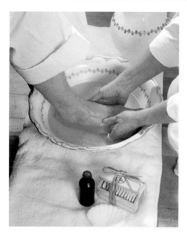

**Step 1** FOOT BATH
Pour warm water into the bowl and, treating one foot at a time, wash thoroughly with either oatmeal soap or your own natural alternative. Use pumice stone to remove any hard skin from the feet and brush off with the bristle brush.

**Aromatherapy Note (optional):**
Add 1 drop each of frankincense, geranium and jasmine to a bowl of warm water. Let your partner soak both their feet in the bowl for 10–15 minutes. Pumice away hard skin, brush and dry as in Steps 1 and 2.

**Step 2** DRYING & CLIPPING
Dry each foot in a warmed towel. Make sure you dry between the toes. Pull each toe in turn to stretch out hidden tensions. Rub the feet either with a lotion, such as peppermint, or talcum powder. Clip the nails, if necessary.

**Step 3** WALKING ON THE SOLES
Right. Have your partner lay on their front on a padded surface with their heels a little apart and relaxed in an open position. Stand on their insteps with your heels and walk up and down from toes to the middle of the insteps.

**Step 4** ANKLE & KNEE STRETCH
Below right. This sequence works on the stomach, spleen, liver and kidney meridians. Kneel at your partner's feet. Part their legs as far as is comfortable. Cross the right leg over the left and clasp the toes with your hands. On your partner's out-breath, push the feet towards the buttocks. Hold for 2–3 complete breaths. Repeat with the left foot over the right. Repeat the whole sequence 2–3 times.

**Finishing Touch:**
Smooth down the legs to relax them, resting with the palms of your hands on the soles of their feet for a minute or so. Then slowly draw your hands off the toes.

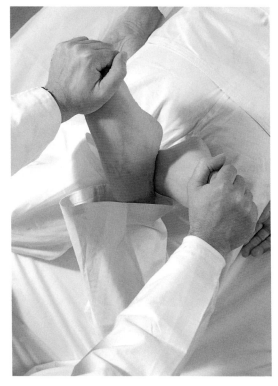

## To Refresh and Revive

There are several types of remedial-style treatments for the feet that can have a dramatic and lasting effect on your health and well-being, e.g. reflexology, Shiatsu, acupressure and general massage.

Reflexology, or zone therapy, as it used to be known, is one of the most popular forms of treatment today. It has been used in Asia for many centuries by physicians and healers alike. This form of foot massage has been used as an aid to diagnosis and treatment of both major and minor health problems. It is increasingly being recognized here in the West by members of the medical profession, interested in allopathy, as a natural, non-drug-related and non-invasive complementary treatment to traditional medicine.

The following easy step-by-step techniques are a valuable introductory preparation to the fuller range of practices which should be studied through a professional body.

**Step 1** Tension Release
Sit facing your partner's feet and rest one foot on your knee. Hold and support their ankle with one hand whilst pulling each toe, in turn, with the other hand. Then, supporting around the ball of the foot, gently pull and circle each toe three times in a clockwise direction. Sandwich the foot between both hands and 'smooth-off' as you pull up and off the toes. Repeat on the other foot.

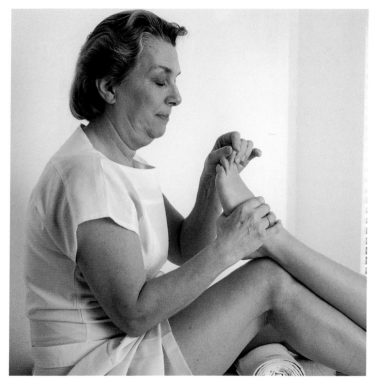

**Note:** a) Keep your eyes on your partner as much as possible in case you touch on any sensitive areas that need extra care and attention.

b) Use either talcum powder or oil for the following massage techniques.

**Step 2** METATARSAL TWIST

A tremendous amount of tension is lodged in the chest, neck and shoulders. The reflexology points that relate to these areas are found below the little toe (shoulders), in the area below the three middle toes on the pad of the foot (lungs/chest) and at the base of the big toe (throat/neck/thyroid).

**a)** Lace your fingers around the little toe and upper part of the foot (as illustrated) and slowly but firmly twist it in an anticlockwise direction to the full extent of movement. Hold for a second or two, ease and release. Repeat 2–3 times.

**b)** Lace your fingers around the ball of the foot and slowly but firmly twist the foot in a clockwise direction to the full extent of movement. Make sure the heel of your hand pulls the little toe and outer edge of the foot towards you. Hold for a second or two, ease and release. Repeat 2–3 times.

Repeat techniques a) and b) on the other foot.

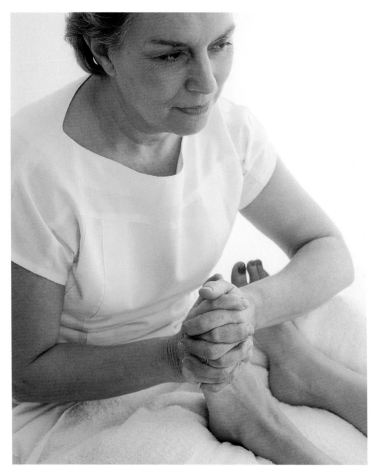

**Step 3** CALF & HAMSTRING STRETCH
**a)** Support your partner's calf on your shin. With the support hand cupped beneath the heel and the working hand clasping the ball of the foot, pull the heel towards you in a gentle traction-type movement to ease the calf muscles. Ease and repeat 3 times.

**b)** Then, changing the position of the upper hand to grasp over the toes, simultaneously push the toes and upper part of the foot away from you whilst pulling the heel towards you. This will give a very strong stretch which should be felt in the hamstring. Do not force this movement. Great sensitivity should be shown with regard to your partner's ability to stretch and move. Repeat 3 times.

**Finishing Touch:** Sandwich the foot between both hands and 'smooth-off' as you pull up and off the toes.

Repeat techniques a) and b) on the other foot.

**Step 4** CATERPILLAR WALK
Wrap your left hand around the toes of your partner's left foot, holding them straight. Work your right thumb, like a caterpillar, from the heel to the little toe. Return to the heel and walk up to the next toe. Repeat for each toe until you walk up the line of the spine to the top of the big toe. If, in the course of this technique, you discover any sensitive points/areas, take a little while to ease and soothe the discomfort before proceeding.

**Finishing Touch:** Sandwich the foot between both hands and 'smooth-off' as you pull up and off the toes.

Repeat the technique on the other foot.

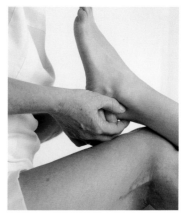

**Step 5** ACHILLES PINCH & PRESSURE STROKE
With the supporting hand cupping the heel, locate the Achilles tendon with the working hand.

**a)** Move up and down the tendon, pinching with the thumb and forefinger. This stimulates the kidney meridian.

**b)** Perform a smooth pressure stroke one either side of the tendon, from heel to the base of the calf, several times. This will improve poor circulation.

c) Reversing the direction of the smooth pressure stroke, from base of calf to heel, will ease out tension around the ankle area.

d) Circle your third and fourth fingers around the ankle bone several times in a clockwise direction. This technique helps to relieve fluid retention problems.

> **Cautionary Note:** Do not work on legs affected with thrombosis or below varicose veins.

Repeat techniques a), b), c) & d) on the other foot.

## Step 6 VALLEYING
Above. Support your partner's foot in your lap.

a) Using the thumb and forefinger of both hands, place your index fingers in the 'valleys', i.e. grooves between the metatarsal bones on the top of the foot. Using a smooth pressure stroke on the outer two valleys between the big and second toe and the little and fourth toe, start halfway up the foot and draw the thumbs down towards

the toes. Simultaneously, draw the forefinger along the sole of the foot. At the end of the stroke, gently pinch between the toes. Release and repeat the procedure on the two inner valleys.

b) Hold and spread the big and second toes with one hand. Using the inside corner of the index finger of the other hand, work up (caterpillar-like) between the metatarsal bones to the middle of the foot. Repeat in the valleys between the other toes, across to the little toe.

**Finishing Touch:** Sandwich the foot between both hands and 'smooth-off' as you pull up and off the toes.

Repeat techniques a) and b) on the other foot.

## Step 7 PRESSURE FLUID RELEASE
Below. Support your partner's foot in your lap. This is an excellent technique for releasing fluid retained around the ankles and feet.

Start at the valley between the Achilles tendon and the ankle bone. Using either the thumbs or middle fingers, make small circular flowing movements as you work your way round under the ankle bone to the top of the foot (as illustrated). Finish with larger circling movements of your middle fingers around both ankle bones. Repeat 3 times.

**Finishing Touch:** Sandwich the foot between both hands and 'smooth-off' as you pull up and off the toes.

Repeat the technique on the other foot.

### To Drain and Detoxify

Cellulite and poor circulation are the bane of many people's lives. They can so easily be alleviated by an improved diet coupled with regular exercise, massage or aromatherapy.

An excellent first step would be reducing (and possibly eliminating) the intake of tea, coffee and canned soft drinks. Replace with still, filtered water. Fresh food that is prepared just before the meal is another prerequisite. Keep to simple meal formats that do not include too many different types of food. Starch and protein, eaten together, are quite difficult for your body to assimilate.

The second requirement of health management is daily exercise. Choose a system such as yoga, Tai Chi or swimming that does not overtax the joints.

Massage and aromatherapy both work on the lymphatic system which helps to eliminate toxins and waste products from the body. There may well be a diuretic effect, so warn your partner that they may wish to visit the bathroom more often as a result of the treatment.

The following techniques can either be performed sitting astride or standing beside the massage couch, or kneeling on the floor. Rest your partner's legs, slightly parted, on your thighs. Do not massage on the inner part of the thigh.

**Step 1** Thigh Gliding

Supporting and strengthening the wrist of the working hand, glide the heel of the palm 6 times up the back and sides of the thigh. Work from just above the back of the knees to the buttocks and the side of the hips just below the hip bone. The pressure should be firm and the movements smooth and rhythmical. Repeat on the other thigh.

**Step 2** Calf & Shin Smoothing

Supporting your partner's feet on your shoulders, place one hand on the sole of the foot and one on the ankle. Smooth down the calf towards the back of the knee, rotate the hands and bring the heels of the palms together either side of the shin bone. With your hands cupped round the leg, push the heels of your hands up the shin and foot to the toes. Rotate your hands back into the

**Aromatherapy Note:** My recommendation for an essential oil blend for the treatment of cellulite: juniper (2 drops), lavender (2 drops), rosemary (2 drops) to 10ml of carrier oil (sweet almond). My recommendation for the treatment of poor circulation: black pepper (2 drops), benzoin (1 drop), marjoram (2 drops), sage (1 drop) to 10ml of carrier oil (sweet almond). Do not use either blend during pregnancy – only carrier oil.

starting position and repeat the sequence three times on both legs.

**Step 3** DRAINING
Below. With your partner's foot free from your shoulder, cup the upper part of the foot in both hands, wrists touching. Press your fingers into the sole of the foot from just below the middle toe. Then, in a straight line, proceed down the sole pressing and releasing roughly every inch (2.5cm). Rest the foot on your shoulder as you work over the heel and down into the valleys either side of the Achilles tendon. From here, the grouped fingers

should exert a smooth, gliding pressure down the calf to an inch or so above the back of the knee. Release the finger hold, rotate the palms and bring the heels, once again, on either side of the shin bone. The return stroke is the same as Step 2. Repeat the sequence 3 times and finish off with one repetition of the smoothing stroke (Step 2).

Repeat the technique on the other leg.

**Step 4** ANKLE & KNEE STRETCH
Below right. This sequence works on the stomach, spleen, liver and kidney meridians. Part your partner's legs as

far as is comfortable. Cross the right leg over the left and clasp the toes with your hands. On your partner's out-breath, push the feet towards the buttocks. Hold for 2–3 complete breaths. Switch the leg positions, with the left foot over the right. Repeat the whole sequence 2–3 times.

**Finishing Touch:** Smooth down the legs to relax them, resting with the palms of your hands on the soles of your partner's feet for a minute or so. Then slowly draw your hands off the toes.

## To Calm, Comfort and Protect During Pregnancy

Pregnancy is a very special time and it is easy to forget your healthy routines, especially if you have other children to look after. Even a growing foetus can pick up on stressful feelings and a bad atmosphere.

Therefore, calming and comforting the senses plays a vital part in bonding with and giving birth to a healthy and happy baby. In addition, touching for health is a key way of protecting yourself from unnecessary stretch marks.

There are numerous naturopathic lotions and oils on the market. It is very much a matter of personal preference which you choose to use in the following routines. Relaxing after a shower or bath is an ideal time to enjoy your own loving touch. Even better, involve your partner in these intimate practices.

**Aromatherapy Caution:** Please take professional advice if you wish to use aromatherapy oils since so many are dangerous or inappropriate to the pregnant condition. However, carefully selected oils, used before, during and after the birth, can be excellent aids to soothe, comfort and protect.

**Step 1** RESTING POSITION
Opposite below. Rest with a rolled bath towel under your knees and 3–4 pillows under your back, shoulders and head. The roll under the knees takes the pressure off the lumbar region.

**Step 2** OILING/LOTIONING
Right. Rub your selection of oils or lotions gently, in a clockwise direction around your abdomen and stomach until they have been absorbed by the skin. Then massage around each breast.

**Step 3** CRADLING & COMFORTING – 8 MONTHS
Below. During pregnancy, whilst the baby's head is uppermost, place your hands above and below its growing form. Visualize loving energies flowing between the poles of your palms and providing energetic nourishment.

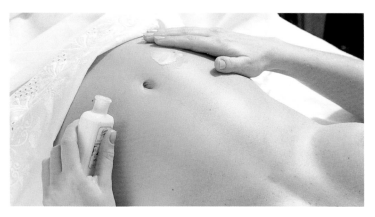

**Step 4** PREPARING FOR THE BIRTH
Below right. When you have felt (or been informed) that the baby has turned and is head down, change the position of your hands and visualize a safe delivery.

# CHAPTER THREE
# MEDITATION

## INTRODUCTION

*This book represents a mere microcosm of the vast and profound corpus that is the literature of meditation. From a maze of inter-cultural and historical possibilities, a small glimpse of the variations and complexities of the human mind can be glimpsed. From one perspective, at least, meditation can be viewed as an antidote to the maladies that affect the distracted mind – as an instrument of healing. From another, it would seem that the devotional or mystical aspects of meditation are a necessary discipline, a source of inspiration and a way of offering praise to the Universal Spirit.*

*Even to define the word 'meditation' we need to reflect on what the word means according to the mind that apprehends it. Even the word 'mind' has a different connotation seen from the Eastern perspective. There, it is more likely to be seen as 'the intelligence of the heart' or 'heart-mind' as distinct from the Western tradition of linking the mind to the brain or intellect.*

*The definition of meditation ranges from systematic reflection upon religious topics, intense interior observation of our thought processes, the act of turning matters over in the mind to reach a solution or simply the desire to mentally*

explore the nature and purpose of the universe. The word also describes the activity of 'exercising' the mind, especially in a devotional sense. This form of meditation can mean serious and sustained reflection or mental contemplation. Its religious application is the contemplation of some religious truth, mystery or object of reverence as an exercise in piety.

According to a Christian view: 'In meditation we converse with ourselves; in prayer we converse with God.' However, we are also urged to recognize that the kingdom of heaven is within.

It seems to be a common view that meditation is a technique, even to be put on cassette, which involves visualization to ambient/New Age music, designed to encourage relaxation and deeper sleep. Meditation with a view towards eventual liberation from suffering, i.e. enlightenment, is a specifically spiritual perspective and is meant to 'wake us up', not to put us back to sleep. So, although there are different forms of meditation, for relaxation, life-evaluation, reprogramming (i.e. giving up smoking), these are only useful preparatory techniques, not to be confused with the ultimate aim of self-realization.

Possibly, in the context of the spiritual path, it would be more useful to say what meditation is not:

- It is not an investigation into the occult or paranormal.

- It is not a blank mind, empty of thought.

- It is not discursive thinking or introspection: it is not hypnosis, a state of suggestibility or trance.

- Rather, we need to break the spell. Meditation can de-hypnotize us and free us from all illusions and dependencies. Using methods derived from empirical techniques applied over thousands of years of human experience, we have a systematic set of techniques for studying our minds and applying discipline to the concentration and will. We will then be able to make the journey from the first layer of consciousness to explore the heights and depths. We have the spiritual technology!

If we can imagine ourselves as tadpoles, swimming around our small pool of ignorance, a person adept at meditation could be seen as a frog leaping into our world with tales of another realm. A little tadpole asks such questions as: 'Well, how do you get around out there?' The frog's description of hopping and jumping would be met with blank incomprehension. 'Well, it's not swimming', the frog would helpfully reply. 'How do you breathe?' enquires the tadpole? The frog, getting the hang of it now, instantly replies: 'Well, not with gills.' 'What do you breathe?' asks another: 'Not water', he says enigmatically! This could continue for some time.

Ramakrishna, the Indian mystic, had this to say of knowledge: 'Later, however, when the tadpole's tail of ignorance drops off, there is the ability to move between these two elements equally for full attainment of its potential.'

The techniques presented in this book are continually exploring the interplay of polarities to bring us to some understanding of the harmony and balance between opposites. For us, the adventure could be to wonder if we could go all the way to heaven, embracing all, and all the way back to hell without identifying with either of them. All it needs is the capacity to be completely involved and completely detached at the same time, life's eternal paradox!

The first question that springs to mind is, 'Why not?' Countless people throughout the world since time immemorial have meditated in one way or another, so it must have something going for it. Moreover, it is recommended, in one form or another, by virtually every religion and belief system.

As many a regular meditator will tell you, there is a sense of 'coming home', of finding something that was precious and previously lost. Lawrence LeShan, in his book, *How to Meditate*, observes: 'We meditate to find, to recover, to come back to something of ourselves we once dimly and unknowingly had and have lost without knowing what it was or where or when we lost it.'

And what is that thing we have lost? It is contact with the full potential of our own selves that we may once have had for a short time as children, if we were lucky. To be tantalized by a thought of something better, and to later on not quite know what is missing, leads to a sense of separation and loss. We suffer, and the strongest motivation to do something about it is to alleviate it if we can.

Meditation can be seen as taking a holiday from the external world, and a journey into oneself. We all need a break now and again, and to one who meditates, that valuable time when one is truly centred within oneself, can bring refreshment to a flagging physical body, battered emotional system and overloaded mind.

It is amazing just how much time people spend on the outward search for an ecstatic union with another. It is most clearly demonstrated by the often desperate (and fruitless) search for a sexual partner to complete what is perceived as a lack in oneself. Jungians describe it as the union of our male and female selves, Animus and Anima. Whether it is acknowledged or not, most people are involved in a desperate search for 'oneness'. The object of meditation is to seek that union within, not to look for outward fixes through external distractions or other people which are temporary measures and will not last the course. We are not talking about a heavenly 'top of the mountain' search but a very real process which brings the benefits of no longer feeling fractured, separate and cut off from the Source (however that might be imagined).

The fruits of meditation can only be realized from the practice of it. Practice can bring you to a place of surrender where a state of grace or the kingdom of heaven within can be achieved. In the external world everything is perceived as linear, measured by time. The meditative state, however, is timeless, exemplified by the statement, Be Here Now.

There are increasing numbers of people in our modern age who have rediscovered the benefits of meditation, and carers and members of the medical profession could be included in this category. On one level there is plenty of scientific research to show the value of meditation-style practices in treating conditions such as high blood pressure and anxiety. They offer a cheaper and safer alternative to drugs without the hazard of side effects. In addition, biofeedback techniques and visualization exercises are increasingly employed to help people suffering from mental disorders.

On another level, carers themselves (doctors, nurses, etc.) are appreciating the benefits meditation can bring. If, on a day-to-day basis, you are required to deal with suffering and death, there comes a point when you have to make sense of it all. If you're in a war zone it is even more difficult to reconcile your dedication to healing to the continuing carnage which surrounds you.

This need to find some underlying rationale to lives that, at some stage, may seem pointless or meaningless, will face almost everyone in the course of their lives, whatever their occupation or lifestyle. When human beings face a personal tragedy, such as the death of a loved one, the question 'why' comes poignantly to the surface. This moment of crisis could be utilized as a point of change, a chance to transform one's life, and meditation offers, in the experience of many, the golden opportunity.

## THE TREE OF LIFE

The purpose of this practice is to enable you to see more clearly where you are in the maze of your life's experiences and to evaluate the options that are open to you.

It can highlight where areas of your life are blocked, but more importantly supplies the answer to the question of where to go next along the path of helping yourself. You will need a large piece of drawing paper, a firm board to mount it on, and various coloured felt-tip pens. There are no rules as to where and when to practise. Just do it when you feel the need for greater clarity or are at the crossroads of an important decision.

## THE PRACTICE

- **Roots:** Draw the roots of the tree and don't worry if you're no great artist, that's not important. On each root fill in, either in the form of pictures, symbols or words, something that comes to mind from your childhood. It may be as trivial or as serious as you like, but be spontaneous.

- **Trunk:** Draw in a trunk and fill in the first thing that comes to mind about your adolescence, i.e. going to college, any specific training you underwent or work you undertook, any interest, friendships or relationships you formed.

- **Branches:** On each branch mark in an experience or achievement in your follow-on years, being as specific as you like.

- **Smaller Branches:** These are your dreams and aspirations, however bizarre they may be. Feel free to put down your innermost thoughts. Be honest with yourself.

- **Fruits:** These are memorable moments or occasions which you would like to record.

Now stand back and look at the general shape of the tree, roots, branches and fruit. See if there are any breaks in connection or if there is a time and place that formed a block or cut the connection with the mainstay of your life. Notice the correlation between your aspirations and your early beginnings. Study it carefully to see any visual messages it has for you. There is usually something. If there isn't, take the time and patience to come back to it at a later date and then see what it has to offer. You are not dwelling on the negative aspects of your life, you are making yourself aware of the potential available to you in the future.

The following are guidelines designed to help you in the initial stages of meditation. You are not required to be pure in body and mind, neither does your environment need to be wholly conducive to the practice of it There will always be some kind of distraction such as an unplanned noise, draught, smell, etc. Do not be put off, accept it as an integral part of the meditation. Just because conditions are not always ideal you should not use this as an excuse to avoid practice!

### PREPARING YOUR ENVIRONMENT

It is not essential to prepare your environment for relaxation and meditation purposes. They can, in fact, be performed anywhere you feel is appropriate, either going to work on the bus or in the local park, etc.

**Place:** In the initial stages, however, you may find it useful to practise in a special part of your home which is conducive to relaxation and meditation where you won't be disturbed. Avoid extremes of temperature and draughts though it would help to have good ventilation. Natural or subdued lighting is preferred and candlelight is essential for certain practices.

You might wish to add a devotional aspect with a picture of a deity or holy person with whom you can identify. This offers a way of further expression and can act as a focal point in the practice of meditation.

### CLEANSING & PURIFICATION PRACTICE

The practice of washing your body can be used as a form of ritual cleansing or purification. You can, if you choose to, think of it as a way of ridding yourself of aspects of your life that cause you distress, e.g. fear, worry, tension, fatigue, etc.

The physical benefits of scrubbing and applying lotions to the body are important. They help remove the dead cells that are constantly forming on the surface of the skin. This prevents the skin from breathing properly and leaves it feeling unnecessarily taut. If you are going to practise relaxation, it is a good idea to have a warm bath or shower beforehand.

There are spiritual cleansing and purification practices which have been used throughout the centuries, e.g, sweat lodges (Native American), meditation under a waterfall (Taoist), Shankaprakshalana (Hindu Yogic), Vajrasattva (Tibetan Buddhist), and baptism (Christian).

### PREPARING YOUR BODY

**Clothes:** Loose-fitting natural fabrics are ideal for meditation. Both for comfort and to allow energy to flow naturally, avoid wearing belts, ties, tights, shoes, jewellery, watches or glasses.

**Intake:** As a general rule in life it would be best to avoid a whole range of stimulants such as coffee, tea, alcohol and recreational drugs. If you do indulge, give yourself ample time for the greater part of the effects to wear off before your practice. Ideally, do your practice in the morning before you start taking stimulating drinks.

A heavy meal before practice can cause drowsiness. Conversely, lack of food can lead to poor concentration. It is a good idea to empty your bladder and bowels before you begin and, ideally, it is best to allow two hours for a full meal to digest and half-an-hour for fluids. This might not always be possible in a busy schedule. However, even if the situation is not perfect, do your meditation practice anyway!

**Physical/mental energies:** If you wish to meditate first thing in the morning it is no good rolling out of bed while you're half asleep hoping to concentrate the mind. Practise gentle stretching exercises, yogasanas, Surya Namaskar (Salute to the Sun) or Tai Chi movements to centre yourself in your physical body. You do not want your heart racing, so nothing too strenuous or aerobic is needed. Alternatively, take a shower.

Conversely, if you are going to meditate when you come home from work, or after a long day, chances are you will be mentally stressed or physically exhausted. This is also likely to prove a distraction. Again, perform some practices designed to unwind or de-stress the physical body and centre the concentration away from the thinking processes.

'magic time' is. Yogis refer to it as Brahmamuhurta and it generally occurs around 4 a.m.

If possible, avoid rushing off after your practice. Take a few minutes to check for muscle cramps; massage your legs and stretch your body

**Duration:** In the initial stages you needn't commit a lot of time to meditation practice. You can build up from as little as ten minutes a day. If you attempt to do too much too soon you might just be setting yourself up to fail.

Preparing Your Posture
The following are basic techniques but if you wish to carry on with advanced practices, go to a qualified teacher.

### Sitting on a chair

* Sit on the front part of the chair with your hips raised above knee height (use a firm cushion if required).
* Legs should be shoulder-width apart, knees in line with the centre of the feet.
* Relax your shoulders. Do not slump, hunch or 'set' them in military fashion.

### Sitting on the floor

There are several options, e.g. a comfortable straight-backed chair is probably the easiest for most Westerners who do not habitually sit cross-legged on the floor. Sitting on a firm cushion in a cross-legged position is fine provided

**Time:** It is generally recognized that there are certain times that are especially auspicious and conducive to meditation; for instance, dawn and twilight, when there is a full and new moon and at the time of the equinoxes. Various cultures, from time immemorial, have recognized the special energetic potential of the interface between the opposites, light and dark, Yin and Yang, tension and relaxation. A short time before sunrise, the 'beat' or atmospheric quality of the earth seems to change. Of course, times vary depending on the country and season but experience will tell you what that the hips are higher than the knees and there is no strain on the joints or spine. The distraction of aching joints for those unpractised or unfamiliar with yogic meditational postures outweighs the benefits.

Meditation postures from the yogic tradition such as Padmasana (Lotus Position) is ideal but not essential. Variations can include Ardha Padmasana (the Half Lotus), and an astride kneeling position using a zafu cushion, one technique used in Japanese meditation (Zazen). The easiest technique for beginners is Sukhasana (Easy Position). Sit with the legs stretched in front of the body. Fold the right foot under the left thigh. Fold the left foot under the right thigh. Place the hands on the knees. Keep the head, neck and back straight.

The traditional meditation positions require the practitioner to sit on the floor which helps 'ground' the energy.

There are a couple of other alternatives such as postural chairs, designed for people with bad backs (where the weight is shared by knees and buttocks) and meditation stools which relieve pressure on hip, knee and ankle joints.

### Hand Positions, in the Chair or on the Floor

The hand positions (mudras) are many and varied and are associated with specific practices which have distinct effects on the energies of the body and mind. Therefore, if you wish to go on to more complicated methods, you must study the traditions in which they are incorporated. Here are two easy methods of relaxing the hands in meditational postures:

- Place your hands, palms down, on the knees.

- **Mudra of Equilibrium:** The wrists lie on the thighs, palms upwards, left hand cradled in the right, little fingers touching the abdomen. The tips of the thumbs touch, forming a straight line, and in the space inside there is room for two eggs. In some traditions the left hand is on top of the right. In others, this is the 'male' position and the reverse is the 'female' position. In the absence of any specific tradition or instruction, use what feels most natural.

If, in the course of your meditation, the thumbs form an upward-pointing 'mountain', then there is too much tension, if a 'valley' then too little alertness. The correct position denotes equanimity.

### Fine Tuning for Any Sitting Practice
- Rest the tip of the tongue naturally on the upper palate on the line between the teeth and the gums. In many spiritual traditions this links the circuit of energy flowing throughout the body. It has the added advantage of slowing down the output of saliva. Continual swallowing during deep or intensive practice would be a distraction. The mouth should be closed without tension.

- If you are drowsy and in danger of nodding off, keep your eyes open. If you are agitated in any way, keep them lightly closed.

- To correct the spine, concentrate on the top of your head. Imagine a silken thread pulling the whole body upwards as though the skull were being suspended from it. Visualize the vertebrae as beads on that thread. Experience the fluidity of movement from such a viewpoint.

- On the in-breath, gently relax the muscles around the body structure, resisting the tendency to sink into the hips and slump. On the out-breath, lean the body fractionally forward. Appreciate the energetic difference.

- As a final, compassionate touch, permit yourself an inner smile.

### Checking the Body Tension
Concentrate your attention on the top of the scalp.

- On the in-breath slightly tense, on the out-breath gently release the tension and allow a sensation or visualize the energy draining downwards through your body.

- Gently work your way through the body, i.e. relax facial tension, neck, shoulders, stomach or any areas of tension stored in the body.

- At the end of the practice, imagine the tension draining into the ground and discharging. The exercise can be intensified by the association of emotions connected in various areas of the body.

- To re-energize your body, breathe in, bringing the energy upwards and through the top of the head, discharging any tension.

- Reverse the procedure and breathe in energy through the top and down through the body. The practice is limited only by your imagination and the time allowed.

By now your body should be in a comfortable position, relaxed and ready to approach the mind practices.

### Preparing your Mind for Meditation

This is a practice for beginners who find it difficult to focus their attention. It is a simple formula which can be done anywhere, anytime, either sitting up or lying in a position of relaxation.

Split-Second Formula: Think to yourself …

- I detach my mind from my family. I think of them and slowly detach, relax and let myself go.

- I detach my mind from my friends. I think of them … detach … relax … and let myself go …

- I detach my mind from my work or chores. I think of them … detach … relax … and let myself go…

- I hear no particular sound … have no particular feelings … time itself seems to be standing still for a split second of peace and rest …

Allow your mind to rest on a razor's edge between total awareness and a deep feeling of relaxation.

### Stabilizing the Breath

Human beings can survive several weeks without food, several days without water, but without fresh air we are helpless. The difference between life and death is a single breath. Air contains not only oxygen but also the life force and energy from the universe (*prana*, Chi or Ki). We receive air through our lungs into every body cell and yet, generally, we breathe superficially, using a mere one-sixth of our lung capacity. Usually, we breathe approximately 15–20 times every minute. This usually decreases during meditation. As the body and mind relax, the breathing automatically and naturally becomes slower and deeper.

Trance states called *jhanas* are often promoted by this calming of the mind. Meditators are often warned that, although an important step, this is not the goal and can prove an obstacle to further progress. Master of meditation, Kalu Rinpoche, observed that 'at worst, tranquillity meditation is like an animal in hibernation', and suggested how this could be used. Like a 'smooth highway on which we drive to arrive at more advanced levels of Tantric meditation'. So, again, we see the vital necessity of establishing a balance between relaxation and mental alertness.

The following practice is designed to stabilize the body and mind energies through concentration on the breath.

- Without altering the breath, but simply observing it, concentrate the mind on the area below the nostrils and on the upper lip. Simply watch and feel the flow of the breath in and out of the body.

- Let the mind relax in this awareness. If thoughts arise, recognize them and let them go. If it is a 'good' or pleasant thought, be aware of the tendency to try and keep it. Recognize this habit, relax and let go. If a 'bad' thought arises, be aware of the tendency to push it away or deny it. Recognize this habit, accept the thought and simultaneously let it go. Return the mind to concentrating on the point of attention already selected. If the attention wanders, recognize the fact and without blame or judgement, gently bring the mind home. Whether the thoughts appear to be faster or slower, accept each one for what it is, another thought, and let that too dissolve.

A common misunderstanding about meditation is that we have to empty the mind. This is an impossible task, for thoughts come to the mind unbidden. For instance, if you tried to remove 'bad' reflections from a mirror or keep only the 'good' reflections you would soon realize the impossibility of the task. The nature of the mirror is to reflect everything, without grasping or refusing. Similarly, the mind can relax and be at peace within our thoughts.

*'The perfect man employs his mind as a mirror, it grasps nothing, it refuses nothing, it receives but does not keep.'*
                                Chuang-Tsu

Another way of viewing this process is as a wish to find our lost peace of mind. Imagine the mind as a pool of water in which we have lost something. If we take a stick and attempt to find what we are looking for, by poking about on the bottom of the pool, all we succeed in doing is stirring up the mud and clouding the water. If we cease to disturb the water, the mud will gradually settle and the water will return to its natural state and we will be able to clearly see again. Any thought could be visualized as a stone dropping into the pool. We could watch the ripples extend from the epicentre and gradually disappear until, gradually, the water becomes as still as a mill pool reflecting an empty sky.

If we are searching for the nature of our true mind it may be helpful to regard it as our inner 'sun'. It radiates its warmth in all directions. If our thoughts are cloudy the sun may be temporarily obscured so that we forget the endless continuation of that radiance. If we attach too much importance to the clouds we may forget that the sun is always there. Our own radiant nature is always there, we simply have to let go of all that is in the way of our understanding this.

The practice of meditation on the breath is a exercise in one-pointedness or concentration. The benefits are many including relaxation of tension of both body and mind, increased ability to concentrate on everyday matters and the clarity of mind to see situations as they truly are, increased tranquillity, acceptance of oneself and an increasing awareness of the illusory nature of thoughts.

### Observations During Practice

- Watch the natural breath as it becomes shallower.

- As the inner tensions of your body relax, you may feel a wave of drowsiness. Draw yourself up out of your spine and allow the wave to flow over your head.

- If your concentration wanes you may find your thoughts dwelling on the past, in which case you may have sunk back into your pelvis. Alternatively, your thoughts may be grasping at the future and your body may well be leaning forward. In order to bring yourself back to the present moment, simply adjust your posture so that your spine is directly in alignment with the crown of your head and you feel as if you are growing out of the base of the spine.

- Like so many of the benefits of relaxation and meditation, the effects are not necessarily evident during practice. The revitalization of body, mind and spirit can show itself in the form of healthy energy either later in the day or even the following day.

'WEAR YOUR WORRIES LIKE A LOOSE ROBE'

It is not possible to send energy through stiff, neglected muscles, so by performing certain preparatory exercises you can help to balance the body's energies. This practice is great fun to do with a friend. It is a good example of the importance of give and take in the practice of exercise. The stretch, release and relax concept is an important one in all sound exercise programmes. Stretching movements need to be followed by periods of relaxation to allow the blood to flow through the stretched muscles.

**Note:** If you don't have a partner, try the chair exercises on page 152.

PRACTICE

**Step 1:** Opposite

Sit squarely facing your partner with your knees bent, feet supporting each other, arms joined and just below shoulder level. Pause for a few rounds of breath. One partner then pulls the other towards them, holding for a few seconds. Reverse the procedure. Repeat the forward and back movements 6 times. Benefit: Eases stiff ankles, knees and hips.

**Step 2:** Above.

The working partner places their insteps over their partner's knees. Hold hands, then arch back to maximum stretch. Hold for a few seconds and reverse the procedure to stretch forward, allowing your partner to arch their back. Repeat the forward and back stretch 6 times. Change positions to give your partner a more advanced stretch.

**Step 3:** Right.

Press the sole of your right foot to your partner's left and stretch up diagonally forward through the arms, hands joined. Hold the stretch for a few minutes and repeat on the other side. Repeat 6 times on alternative legs.

**Step 4:** Below
Rest back to back for a few minutes to warm the muscles in the back.

**Step 5:** Opposite
Press the soles of both feet to your partner's and extend both your legs up between your arms, simultaneously arching them forwards and backwards, bending the knee, if necessary. Hold the balance for 2–3 minutes, gently extending your legs and spine. There are numerous variations on this theme; try to experiment (perhaps to some music) so that the rhythms of the movements come more easily.

Many of our physical tensions manifest themselves in our backs. We lose more working days due to back problems than to any other complaint. The following exercises are an introduction to relaxation. They help to stretch out the tensions that form in the back muscles either side of the spinal column. They have the added advantage of strengthening the muscles which help to support the spine and prevent the problem of slipped disks.

**Step 1:** Left
Lie down on the floor with your legs resting on a chair. With a folded blanket under your torso, but not under the head, rest for a few minutes to allow the back muscles to 'melt' into the ground. Rest your hands just below the navel.

**Step 2:** Above
Hold onto the front legs of the chair and tilt it slightly back, placing your feet on either arm or on the seat. Simultaneously pull the legs of the chair to the floor while raising the hips, knees open, chin towards the chest. Keep the hips contracted but the diaphragm relaxed. Breathe naturally through the nose, allowing your chest to expand with each incoming breath. Hold for 2–3 minutes. Tilt the chair back and lower the body into the starting position by pressing the muscles of the back firmly into the ground.

**Step 3:**

Rest for 2–3 minutes with arms either above your head or in the starting position. Repeat Steps 1–3 several times according to your own capabilities. Ensure the chin is always at right-angles to the chest and don't clench your teeth.

**Note:** People with high blood pressure or heart problems should only practise Steps 1, 3 and 4.
**Additional Benefits:** Helps regulate the metabolism.

**Step 4:**
Right. Turn the chair around and tilt it to rest your legs on the diagonal. Allow the blood to flow freely down the legs. Rest for a few minutes before going on to the next step.

**Step 5:**
Left. Push the chair legs to the floor, simultaneously pushing yourself up into the shoulder stand position. Rest your feet on the chair back, shoulder-width apart. Keep your breathing natural, your hips contracted and your diaphragm relaxed. Hold for 2–3 minutes, if possible, working up to 15 minutes when you have become more proficient. Rest for 2–3 minutes.

The best-known form of moving meditation is the sacred dance which occurs in most cultures. Many of the dances enact stories and moral tales originating from the great religions: others re-create the world of spirits, flora and fauna. Common to both is the element of meditation present in these dances which in some cases is thought to actually lead to possession. It takes years of arduous training even for the specially gifted to achieve a state of transcendence of the ordinary and the ability to inspire an audience with a sense of the divine

It is possible to gain some concept of this type of meditation by following an exercise such as the simple re-creation of the life of a lotus. The lotus has always been a symbol of spiritual growth: it grows out of the darkness of the mud, through the medium of water to eventually bloom in air and sunlight. The chakras of the energetic centres of the Yogic and Tantric traditions are often referred to as lotuses. While attending to the techniques and positions of the practice, open your heart and mind to the underlying symbolism of rebirth.

*To see a World in a grain of sand,*
*And a Heaven in a wild flower,*
*Hold Infinity in the palm of your hand,*
*And Eternity in an hour.*
William Blake

### THE LOTUS LILY
(for children and the young at heart)
This moving meditation is a practice taken from Yogarhythm. It was specifically arranged for children to give them an insight into meditation through simple visualization techniques.

**Step 1:** The lotus lily starts its day in stillness ...

**Step 2:** As the sun comes up, the petals open ... and by midday its face is smiling towards the sunshine ... drawing in light and energy through its petals, through its stem to the roots.

**Step 3:** The gentle breeze sways the plant from one side ...

**Step 5:** ... to its still centre.

**Step 4:** ... to the other, but always returns ...

**Step 6:** There are many tiny fish swimming around in the water.

**Step 7:** They swim in and around the roots of the plant …

**Step 8:** … to the bottom of the pool.

**Step 9:** There are all kinds of insects and birds …

**Step 10:** ... that hover overhead and come to rest on the lotus lilies.

**Step 11:** The sun goes down and the petals of the lily fold upwards.

**Step 12:** ... closing tightly to seal in the inspiration of the day ...

**Step 13:** ... and rest peacefully until dawn.

## YOGA NIDRA:
## CONSCIOUS RELAXATION WITH
## INNER AWARENESS

Many leading physicians are now convinced that modern ailments and premature ageing are caused by an inability to deal with stress. Understanding and dealing with the causes is an important part of preventive treatment.

Most of us have forgotten how to relax. We once knew it instinctively as babies but gradually forgot as we became adults and the pace and pressure of modern living began to wear us down. If you have a tendency to over-intellectualize, learn to tune into the emotional and intuitive side of your nature by being more open and receptive to your heart centre. For those who consider relaxation and meditation a mere hobby or distraction, consider the basic truth underlying all spiritual practices: death is the only certainty. The moment of death is uncertain, so don't waste this precious life. This need not be a morbid preoccupation but could be used as the best reason for living our lives more usefully. To ease tension and stress is to lengthen and strengthen our lives.

The following practice, Yoga Nidra, was formulated by Paramahansa Satyananda based on the little known but very important Tantric practice of Nyasa. The systematic rotation of consciousness can induce complete physical, mental and emotional relaxation.

Ordinarily, when you lay down to sleep and dissociate yourself from sensory input, the inclination is to fall asleep. This practice, calling for special concentration and awareness, can help you to experience that space between sleep and wakefulness. This is where contact with the subconscious and unconscious dimensions of the mind can be made.

Modern psychology calls this heightened state of sensitivity and awareness the 'hypnogogic state'. This can be a starting point from which to tackle a wonderful range of opportunities such as fast language learning. Once the process of intellectualization is bypassed, information can enter the mind which is likely to be more efficiently retained. The power of suggestion can be more effective at this time, helping us to reject destructive habits and tendencies which are causing havoc in our lives. Your true nature and integrity will come to the fore enabling you to live in peace with your environment. Yogis have used this method of introspection since time immemorial to bring them face to face with their inner selves.

The following section can be recorded on a cassette tape to enable you to establish the pattern until the sequence can be remembered and mentally repeated. Alternatively, ask a friend to guide you through the prac-

tice until you are familiar with it. Do not change the routine once the pattern has become set in the mind.

Remember, the object is to stay awake and aware throughout the practice. Do not be discouraged if you fall asleep the first few times; persevere until you can regularly achieve this state.

YOGA NIDRA – THE PRACTICE

Lie on your back in yoga position Savasana (Corpse Posture). Rest your arms freely by your sides, palms uppermost, arms straight but not rigid, in a natural diagonal line away from your body. Relax your fingers and let them curl naturally into the palms. Make sure your head is in alignment with your feet, legs slightly parted, feet falling open from the hips. Gently close your eyes and keep them closed. Your breathing should be natural and through your nose. There should be no physical movement during the practice.

Now is the time to make a Sankalpa (Resolution). It should be a matter of immense importance to you.

A resolve is a short, positively-worded statement of intent. On one level it might be: 'I resolve to take regular exercise' or 'I resolve to stop smoking'. On a spiritual level it might be: 'I will become more aware' or 'I will be kinder to all beings'. It should be used regularly during your Yoga Nidra practice and should, ideally, be undertaken daily. The realization of such resolves can change your life.

Be aware of your whole body from head to toe: be completely still. Once settled into your position do not move physically.

Starting at the right thumb, repeat mentally the name of each part of the body in the sequence outlined. As you name the body part, simultaneously become aware of it, mentally releasing and relaxing:

Right-hand thumb ... second finger ... third finger ... fourth finger ... little finger ... palm of the hand ... back of the hand ... wrist ... forearm ... elbow ... upper arm ... shoulder ... armpit... side of the body ... hip... thigh... knee ... back of the knee ... shin ... calf ... ankle ... heel ... sole ...

instep ... big toe ... second toe ... third toe ... fourth toe ... little toe.

Become aware of the left-hand thumb ... second finger. ... third finger ... fourth finger ... little finger ... palm of the hand ... back of the hand ... wrist ... forearm ... elbow... upper arm ... shoulder ... armpit ... side of the body ... hip ... thigh... knee... back of the knee ... shin ... calf ... ankle ... heel ... sole ... instep ... big toe ... second toe ... third toe ... fourth toe ... little toe.

Now focus your attention on the back. Become aware of the right shoulder-blade ... the left shoulder-blade ... the right buttock, the left buttock ... the spine ... the whole back together.

Now focus your attention on the top of the head ... the forehead ... both sides of the head ... the right eyebrow ... the left eyebrow ... the space between the eyebrows, the right eyelid, the left eyelid, the right eye, the left eye, the right ear, the left ear, the right cheek, the left cheek, the chin, the throat, the right side of the chest, the left side of the chest, the middle of the chest, the navel, the abdomen.

Now focus your attention on the right leg ... the whole of the left leg ... both legs together (pause). The whole of the right arm ... the whole of the left arm ... both arms together (pause). The whole of the back, buttocks, spine, shoulder-blades ... the whole of the front, abdomen, chest ... the whole of the back and front together ... the whole of the head ... the whole body together ... the whole body together ... the whole body together.

Repeat the process, perhaps once or twice, slowing down with each repetition.

Once your body has been stilled and you have crossed the line where you would ordinarily fall asleep you may, for the first time ever, be aware of 'who you are', existing in a state of consciousness not attached to or defined by the body. In fact, at this stage you should be scarcely aware that you have a body.

Once your awareness has been withdrawn from the senses (Pratyahara – Sense of Withdrawal) then, rather like a freshly popped bottle of champagne, your mind will be flooded with thoughts. This may be particularly true if it is the first time you have opened yourself up to this level of inner awareness.

You may perceive 'good' thoughts and 'bad' thoughts or any range of images produced by the subconscious or unconscious mind. Do not be frightened by or drawn into them. Imagine you are watching a movie displayed on a screen behind your closed eyes (Chidakasha – the Space of Consciousness). Do not be tempted to get drawn into attractive thoughts (happy memories, fantasies, etc.) or try to suppress unpleasant thoughts (negative views of yourself, feelings of anger, etc.), 'treat those two imposters just the same'. Be an observer. In time, if you continue to work with visualization or concentration techniques, the flood of thoughts will subside to a steady trickle and will eventually be only occasional visitors

This 'clearing' aspect of the Yoga Nidra technique is extremely valuable and is similar to the clearing process that goes on in the brain during REM (rapid eye movement) sleep. It is a necessary function of the human brain and therefore quite natural. The difference is that you are conscious and aware of the process. It has often been said that half-an-hour of Yoga Nidra is worth 3 hours' sleep. If you work long hours when you are denied sleep, use this technique to facilitate the necessary clearing process.

The process of Yoga Nidra ends at this point with the three-fold repetition of your resolve. Visualize your face as you see it in a mirror. See your whole body lying on the floor and, once more, become aware of the physical body. Slowly start to move your fingers and toes and stretch gently and slowly. Open your eyes and sit up.

*The practice of Yoga Nidra is complete.*

Since the dawn of mankind the medium of sound has, in both its sacred and profane forms, been used for healing and meditational purposes. Many of our more ancient cultures, such as pre-Christian, Chinese, Tibetan, Indian, Australian Aboriginal, Native American, South American, Polynesian, etc., have preserved the most important elements, linking sound to breath, vibration to internal organs and the chanting of 'revealed' or sacred names in paeans of praise and worship.

We are all familiar with the spectacle of sporting events enlivened by chants and songs. Singing with a choir or group is a form of group consciousness which allows the individual, for a short time, to forego their individuality and, through this temporary phenomenon, obtain a feeling of great release. This could be seen as a modern-day equivalent of the pagan Saturnalia or tribal gathering. In the presence of charismatics, evangelical preachers, Pentecostal or gospel churches, the effects can be both dramatic and liberating.

In the healing arts, sounds have long been ascribed to both physical organs and their energetic, non-physical counterparts, the *chakras* (wheels/lotuses). They are amenable to manipulation by skilled practitioners and attunement through self-regulation.

The very first expressive use of

musical sound by human beings almost certainly manifested itself in the drum beat. Musicians, and drummers in particular, have always known that sound and rhythm can alter human consciousness. A rhythm that mimics the heart rate will 'entrain' it. Slowly increasing the rhythm will speed up the heart to a pitch of excitement and sometimes explosive release. This technique has been cynically used by extremist political groups, for sensory pleasure at pop concerts and raves, and for spiritual purposes by religious groups.

Most spiritual cultures take the view that the universe is a projection of sound vibrations alone. Muslim (Sufi) saints have said that the world evolved from sound and form and the Bible states: 'In the beginning was the Word (sound), and the Word was with God and the Word was God.' Modern science concurs that everything in the universe is nothing more than the continual interplay of vibrational energy and sound is no more than a particular form of vibration. As Paramahansa Satyananda points out: 'Yoga philosophy maintains that even the different layers of mind and body, gross and subtle, are nothing but the manifestation of an uncountable number of different sound vibrations in a multitude of permutations and combinations. We can say that the mind and the body are the solidification of sound.'

## THE NAME OF GOD

Every culture has a name for God as the Supreme Ground of Consciousness or Love or Awareness, however the Divine is described. These names are sometimes 'revealed' to saints, sages, holy men, prophets and shamans (native healers) who have directly experienced them in superconscious states. The Yogic and Tantric traditions maintain that the names of God are the nearest vocal equivalent to a much more subtle sound. By the repetition and chanting of names such as Jesus Christ, Rama, Krishna and Shiva, Allah, etc., one can bring one's consciousness into sympathetic resonance with the divine energies. What initially start out as vocal sounds are eventually interpreted by the mind in a far more subtle way. Rather like cranking up a generator or winding up a spinning top, the momentum will start to carry the practitioner along. This leads to identification with the divine and, sometimes, to expression of those qualities associated with it.

Hymn singing is the most obvious Christian practice while repetition of the Koran (Muslim) or the Bhagavad Gita (Hindu) are both well-known and respected practices.

## THE MANTRA

A mantra is a potent sound or series of sounds which are used to induce an altered state of consciousness. The word 'mantra' is from the Sanskrit noun *manas* which pertains to mind in conjunction with the verb root *tra*, meaning to protect. Simple repetitions of mantras, while going about one's everyday tasks, protect the mind from wandering and disturbing thoughts. This is especially efficacious when used in conjunction with rosary beads, prayer or worry beads and *malas* where physical and vocal repetition is combined.

On another level, mantras can be used as energetic tools, potent symbols that can be used to shock, calm and stimulate energetic blocks within oneself or others. This requires a high level of understanding and experience and would usually be utilized by a spiritual teacher on a prepared pupil, a healer on a patient, or a martial artist on an opponent (the famed Japanese 'Kiai' that can momentarily paralyse). Conversely, from the same tradition, meditation is vital to truly understand that silence is a prerequisite before the mind and body can recover their natural unity.

*Out of silence rises up*
*the Immortal Spirit.*
In the same way that movement comes from stillness, the cry of the spirit rises out of silence.

### MEDITATIONAL PRACTICE
**Aum or Om Chanting**
OM MANI PADME HUM is one of the best known of mantras, commonly translated as 'Precious Jewel in the Lotus' and often referred to as the Mantra of Compassion in the Buddhist tradition. It has many uses, ranging from a simple method of protection for the mind to a spiritual dynamic producing profound insights into outer, inner and supreme realizations. 'OM', in this context, represents the body and externally purified negative actions. Internally, it purifies all perceptions and the subtle channels. The depth of knowledge involved in even one such mantra is vast and a subject worthy of study in its own right.

Instruction from a teacher of recognized provenance and experience is necessary if you wish to use visualization to realize the full potential of the mantra. However, you will be able to gain some first-hand experience by practising the following technique.

Chant the mantra OM or, more correctly, AUM. This sacred sound is universally recognized as a beneficial resonance. It recurs in the main religions, to Jews and Christians as 'Amen', to Muslims as 'Amin' and to Hindus and Buddhists as 'Aum'. It is the most fundamental of sounds reproduced by the human voice when exhaling from abdomen, rib cage and chest in a complete breath.

- Inhale, expanding first the abdomen to draw air deep into the lungs. As you continue inhaling, the rib cage expands and finally you fill the chest.

- Exhale slowly by contracting the abdomen and sounding the syllable Aaaaaaaaaaaaa. As you contract the rib cage the sound should change to Ooooooo. Finally there should be a trailing off of resonance in the upper chest and resonance in the nasal cavities of Mmmmmm. The three sounds should gently merge one into the other. AaaaaaOoooooooMmmmmrnm.

- Repeat as many times as you wish.

### KIRTAN
Kirtan is a form of devotional singing using mantras which contain the names of God. The most familiar is likely to be the Maha Mantra (Great Mantra) of Hare Krishna, Hare Krishna, Krishna Krishna, Hare Hare, Hare Rama, Hare Rama, Rama Rama, Hare Hare. Om Namah Shivaya and its variations are also very well known. Repetition with the mind and heart on the object of one's devotion is the key to this process. Singing, drumming with mridanga and tabla, and the hand-pumped harmonium are the traditional instruments which accompany this form of devotional practice.

### NADA YOGA
**'The Flow of Consciousness' –**
**Sound**
Nada Yoga originates from the Yogic, Tantric and Sufic traditions which are

part of a worldwide spiritual culture, not specifically confined to one location, religion or belief system. The following techniques are methods of penetrating the deeper layers of the mind using sound as a medium. They are excellent practices for inducing Pratyahara (Sense of Withdrawal) and states of meditation.

They will calm and de-stress an overactive, overtaxed or worried mind.

There is a theory that every individual body produces its own unique sound. If we allow ourselves to experiment with subtle sound it offers a way to become attuned and in harmony with the natural vibrations of our body, speech and mind.

Beginners should practise in a place and at a time when external sounds are at a minimum. Late at night or early in the morning are especially recommended. There is no set duration for this practice although 15 minutes is the minimum to gain any effect. Regularity of practice is the key to fruitful experience.

### BHRAMARI PRANAYAMA
### Humming Bee Breathing

- Sit comfortably, in a chair or on the floor, with your head, neck and spine in a straight line. Let your breathing be relaxed, calm and natural.

- Inhale, tuck your chin into your neck and hold the breath for as long as is quite comfortable.

- Raise your chin, gently close your ears with your fingers, and exhale with a continuous, unforced humming note. You will feel a very pleasant vibration in your head and chest.

- Repeat for as many breaths as you wish. Sit quietly after your practice and listen for the subtle reverberations.

### MEDITATIONAL PRACTICE:
### Nada Yoga

- Squat on a rolled-up blanket or large cushion, keeping this beneath the buttocks and between the legs. The cushion should be high enough so that the back is not cramped. Rest your elbows on your knees, place your fingers on the top of your head and seal the ears gently with the thumbs.

- Relax the whole body. Keep the teeth slightly separated and the mouth closed.

- Inhale deeply and, while exhaling, produce a humming sound like a bee. Feel it vibrate throughout the head, starting from the base of the throat (5 minutes).

- Stop humming and listen for subtle sounds. Keep listening for any sound. One will become clearer and clearer. Keep your mind totally on this sound. Listen with intensity.

- As your hearing ability becomes more sensitive you will be able to detect another sound in the background, behind the predominant one.

- Leave the first sound and concentrate on the emerging one. Eventually you will be able to hear yet another sound behind the second. Again concentrate on this third sound and bring it to the fore.

- Carry on in this manner, searching for ever more subtle sounds. The more subtle the sound, the deeper you delve into the mind.

Don't be discouraged if you can't hear the subtle sounds at first, practice and attunement may take time. The sounds you may perceive depend very much on your personality and cultural background since so much is a relative interpretation. When outer sounds and inner sounds cease to distract, we find a paradox emerging, described in the Buddhist tradition as 'The Roaring Silence'.

**Chun Fu/Inner Truth**
This symbol, shown on the wall in the picture on the right, expresses the truth and origins of spirituality. In the figure, two broken lines (Yin-feminine) lie between two solid lines (Yang-masculine). This denotes emptiness within form and represents a pure, open and empty mind, a heart free of prejudice and therefore open to truth.

Joyousness and gentleness are the attributes of two primal trigrams: Tui means joyousness in following the good and Sun means penetrating into the hearts of men.

*'... Inner Truth and Perseverance to further one. Thus man is in accord with heaven.'*
'I Ching', translated by Richard Wilhelm

Body awareness is one of the first steps in the practice of relaxation. Muscles automatically relax when the mind is resting and the emotions stilled.

It is possible for a great deal of energy to drain away if you don't have periods of relaxation. By conserving energy, the body and mind can achieve a state of tranquillity and serenity.

It is easy to become accustomed to the fact that one is lacking in energy and in a perpetual state of nervous agitation. This causes blood vessels to contract, hampering the release of impurities from the body and increases susceptibility to disease or illness. Relaxation is truly the elixir of life. The various methods enable you to meet each day with the spirit of a mild spring breeze rather than that of a whirlwind. By regular practice you will be able to naturally balance any tendencies towards depression, anxiety or over-excitement in your daily life.

To live in a state of tranquillity can be compared to the calm, still surface of the water reflecting the moon and a flying bird. It neither grasps the one nor rejects the other. True living calm is the mind that reflects with equanimity.

### STANDING PRACTICES
*(to help calm the mind and steady the body)*

Unlike Yoga, Tai Chi Ch'uan is performed with the body upright (Basic Stance for many martial arts).

- Stand with your feet parallel, shoulder-width apart, with the weight equally distributed. The skeleton hangs as though suspended from the crown of the head.

- Relax through the joints so that the body's weight sinks downwards and 'roots' through the feet.

- Allow your arms to hang freely by your sides.

- Stand quietly, breathing naturally and allow the body to recognize its connection to the earth.

- Rest the tongue on the line between the upper teeth and the palate. Relax the face in a subtle inner smile.

### WATERFALL MEDITATION
*(for purifying the body and mind)*

Imagine you are standing under a waterfall. A stream of water gently cascades over your head, running downwards over the outside of your body, taking with it tensions and negativities. These soak harmlessly into the ground.

Repeat three times.

Imagine that the water is entering the crown of the head (*bai hui*), and its cleansing force is running through the inside of your body. Use your imagination to visualize the cleansing of the organs, joints, digestive tract, etc. The water drains the negativities and toxins out of the body which pass through the soles of the feet and into the earth.

Note: The temperature of the water can be imagined as hot, cold or warm, depending on the climate and whether you are feeling over- or under-stimulated.

### MEDITATION WITH THE BREATH
*(for unifying our energy with the universe)*

The universe is a limitless circle with a limitless radius. Condense this into One Point and centre it on the lower T'antien (Field of Immortality) which is the centre of our universe.

To find this centre, adopt Basic Stance as before, with the first three fingers of the left hand underneath the navel. Take the index finger of the right hand, place it in line with the navel, underneath the fingers, pointing towards the spine. Imagine a small sphere of condensed energy resting just in front of the spine.

This is the physical centre of the body's gravity and also the meeting point of ascending energy from the earth (Yin) and descending energy from the sky (Yang). The dynamic interplay of the 'marriage of opposites' is the internal alchemical marriage of the male/female energies of the universe. This is the source of the vital energy which keeps the practitioner healthy and leads to an extended, useful life.

In Taoism, the inspiration for practice comes from the belief that we have evolved sufficiently to need but one human rebirth. The ultimate 'attainment' is to become 'an Immortal', one who has transcended birth and death. In Hinduism and Buddhism the theory of reincarnation states that a dedicated enough follower can be released from the cycle of birth, death and rebirth in one lifetime. Those of lesser achievement can work towards a future rebirth and in the process receive more support, i.e. a strong body, supportive parents, access to spiritual teachings, etc.

Many of the various martial/spiritual disciplines from the East contain a synthesis of Taoist, Buddhist and Confucianist beliefs. The 'long life' practices which spring from the Taoist viewpoint that we should make the best use of this precious opportunity that is human life, affords the best chance of realization. Free from the distractions of ill health and motivated

170

by this premise we can endeavour to gain insight into the age-old questions Who Am I? Where did I come from? Why am I here? and Where am I going? Many of the mind techniques in advanced practices deal with this question from the viewpoint of 'Who is this I?'

### THE PRACTICE

- Relax into Basic Stance. Breathe naturally for a few moments.

- Extend the out-breath so that it travels infinitely to the ends of the universe.

- Breathe in so that your breath reaches your One Point (T'antien) and continues infinitely.

- Repeat for at least 5 minutes and no longer than 15 minutes initially. Increase at your own discretion.

This Chi breathing method is a simple and important way of unifying mind and body.

- At night, when all is quiet and calm, do this alone and you will feel that you are the universe and the universe is you.

### BENEFITS

You will be led to the Supreme Ecstasy of being One with the Universe. At this moment, the life power that is rightfully yours is fully activated.
(With acknowledgement to the Ki sayings of Koichi Tohei, Aikido Master.)

### MOVING MEDITATION

The method of Tai Chi Ch'uan originates from, and is generated by stillness.

*'The mind should come first and the body later'*

*'The body should follow the mind as a shadow follows an object'*

*'All movements are directed by the mind, not by exerting muscular strength'*

These quotes from the masters show the importance of a concentrated mind in a relaxed body.

To say 'relax' is to poorly translate the often repeated Chinese command, Sung. A Chinese Master, at a loss to communicate this instruction to his pupils, dropped all attempts at verbal explanation and mimed the following: He pretended to take an imaginary piece of heavy elastic between his hands. Grunting and straining, he pulled his hands about a foot apart. Eyes bulging and breathing heavily, he maintained this grip for a few moments. With a relieved sigh he then slowly relinquished his stretching with the words: 'Sung, Sung', as his hands relaxed back to the original position. From his point of view, most Westerners carry this amount of tension with them without any real awareness of its presence. Relaxation is therefore a natural state to which we can return, not one which we need to acquire. Hence, the frequently-heard 'investment in loss' while learning Tai Chi Ch'uan.

It is impossible to give a description and teaching of the moving Tai Chi form in this book. The following exercise will, however, give a taste of the feeling of movement originating not from muscular force, but from internal energy combining breathing and thought.

The paradox, 'effortless effort', is experienced by cultivating a continual letting go and surrender of ego and the giving up of unwanted tension.

From the pages of the Tao Ti' Ching comes this description of the philosophy of Wu Wei on the subject of non-action:

*'Less and less is done until non-action is achieved. When nothing is done, nothing is left undone. The world is ruled by letting things take their course. It cannot be ruled by interfering'*

This is the antithesis of the attitude expressed in our scientific, technologi-

cal society. The Way of Tao is to harmonize with the forces of Nature, not to conquer them. Meditation provides us with an opportunity to listen, in quietness, to our innate, natural saneness – an alternative to our tendency to control our 'body-vehicles' rather than working in friendship with our physical being.

### A Taste of Tai Chi Ch'uan
- Stand in Basic Stance (as previous exercise).

- Close your eyes, concentrating on the breath, allowing it to naturally slow down and deepen.

- Extend your awareness to include the whole body.

- On the in-breath, imagine the breath filling the whole body.

- On the out-breath, imagine the body emptying.

- On each exhalation, feel your hands and arms swell out and float away from the sides of your body.

At first, the movements are subtle and small, but as the practice progresses the feeling is that they are effortless and come from the inside out. This is the physical embodiment of Wu Wei's teaching, non-acting, non-doing. The unification of body and breath rises and falls like the natural rhythm of a calm ocean.

- You can extend this movement gradually, breathing in as you raise the arms and out as you relax them down by your sides.

Concentrate your mind entirely on the sensation of 'allowing' the arms to float upwards, assisted by the breath. Allow them to relax and respond to the gravitational pull on the out-breath. Experience the willingness of the body to follow the gentle guidance of the mind.

Contrast this with the unaware actions of our everyday movements. The brain/mind orders the vehicle of the body around, often with little regard to its innate intelligence. With a spirit of friendly co-operation between mind and body the 'enemy within' has been recognized and embraced. This is the beginning of the wisdom of 'martial heart' activity and the beginnings of compassion!

The arrogance of the intellect is one of the greatest enemies of the martial artist. In the Eastern system of grading, the white belt denotes the student beginner. He or she then rises through the ranks, eventually gaining the prized black belt. After attaining further grades, the Master once more wears the white belt. This exercise in humility is reflected in the saying: 'Zen Mind, Beginner's Mind'.

If you have come to this book and these practices thinking that you cannot do these meditations, that you are only a beginner, be thankful. This is the most useful approach – even if you're an expert!

These methods are useful for concentrating the mind to a focus of single-pointedness. Imagine the sun's rays caught by a magnifying glass. Think of the effect of the concentration of these rays onto a point on a piece of paper. After a time, the paper will scorch and finally burst into flames. When the mind is supremely focused, who knows to what extent latent power can be realized.

There are two main methods, the external or 'object of meditation' and the internal, focus, image or visualization.

### External Practices Using an Object

Many objects are classically used for meditational purposes: depending on the system of belief, culture and intention, these can vary immensely. An object of religious contemplation can be used as a means of channelling concentration, such as the elaborate iconographical representations of different aspects of consciousness. These can include the pantheon of deities or avatars of Eastern systems (as well as those associated with Christianity) together with the simple geometric representations (*yantra*) of cosmic forces. The image may represent the embodiment of an abstract quality such as Compassion (Chen Rezig) in a Tibetan Buddhist *t'ankha* (painting) which can be used as a Tantric meditational device to 'realize the emptiness

of all phenomena'. Whatever object of meditation is used and from whatever culture, it is still possible to reach a common goal, even if they are along different routes of understanding. Depending on form and colour, different images can evoke varying changes of consciousness and states of awareness in the mind of the practitioner.

Other objects that can be included in this meditation: a flower, a stone, everyday object, a living candle flame, moving water (the latter two a little more difficult). In the advanced practices of Dzogchen, the gaze rests in the Infinite Space of the Sky, the most subtle external object.

### CANDLE MEDITATION
### TRATAKA
*'There is a healing light shining in the centre of my being'*

* The word Trataka means to gaze steadily. It is one of the best-known practices to develop power of concentration and memory. It has the additional benefit of strengthening eye muscles, thus improving eyesight.

### PRACTICE

* Sit comfortably either on the floor or in a chair (see Preparations for Relaxation & Meditation).

* Place a candle at arm's length and at eye level, directly in front of

the body when in a sitting position, and light it.

* Close your eyes and become aware of the whole body. Make any necessary adjustments so that you will not need to move during the practice.

* Open your eyes and gaze at the brightest part of the flame, just above the wick. Your eyes should be wide open, though without strain. Try not to blink if you can help it. With practice this will get easier, but if you feel real discomfort, blink gently, then continue with your practice. Do not move the pupils.

* If your mind wanders, gently bring it back. Do this for three minutes, then close your eyes. Visualize the after-image of the candle flame at the centre between the eyebrows (Bhrumadhya).

* Practice for as long as the image is clear. If any thoughts arise, then simply be a witness to them.

* Open your eyes again and focus on the candle flame for about three minutes.

* Close your eyes again and concentrate on the inner image.

- Repeat this process of outer gaze and inner visualization for as long as you wish. Finally, keep your eyes closed and be a witness to your thoughts. Open your eyes and extinguish the candle.

An alternative way of using an object for meditational practice is to use it simply as a reference point in order to witness or observe the way the mind reacts when focused upon it. The following practice is a starting point to exercise the mind. In the same way that a physical work-out in a gymnasium (if done skillfully) can strengthen the body and increase flexibility, these mind practices will enable the mind to be stretched and focused. It is important to avoid indulging in mere 'mental gymnastics' but to proceed with a clear understanding of our motivation.

These are preparations to loosen up the tensions of habitual mind patterns that may not be serving us usefully. A well-balanced work-out should have the result of healthily relaxing our body or mind (preferably a synthesis of both).

### MEDITATION PRACTICES
*'The Great Square Has No Corners'*
This is a quotation from a well-known and respected text called the Tao Te Ching, a 6th-century Chinese classic by Lao Tsu. To describe the philosophy of The Tao (The Way) is a virtually impossible task. Consider the fol-

lowing: 'The Tao which can be told is not the eternal Tao. The Name that can be Named is not the Eternal Name'. You can see the problem!

This paradox is also echoed in the Native American view of Wakan Tanka, originally translated as 'Great White Spirit', or even more simply 'Great Spirit'. The more profound and accurate translation is 'Great Mystery', leading us again and again to the futility of trying to express the inexpressible. What can we learn from this? Maybe that an ordinary or finite consciousness attempting to name the Infinite can only point a finger along the Path. The real understanding is to be found alone and in silence. Therefore, any meditational device could be seen as a trick to trap the unwary ego into letting go its death grip on the True Mind.

With this in 'mind', the following practice could be provoking.

### PRACTICE
*'The Great Square Has No Corners'*
Contemplate this simple sentence. Sit in a comfortable meditational posture, close the eyes and, with relaxed breath, repeat this phrase a few times, focusing your attention on it and observing what arises. It can be done either audibly or silently.

This could be viewed as an internal focus of attention. Whatever arises, simply accept and move on.

### PRACTICE
*'The Great Square Has No Corners.'*
MEDITATION ON AN EXTERNAL OBJECT

- On a piece of plain white card, draw an outline of a square in black. Make it whatever size you feel is appropriate for an object of contemplation. Experience the physical creation of this shape.

Drawing can be a meditation exercise in its own right. Try to execute the drawing with efficiency and give it your full attention.

- Sit in a comfortable meditational position with the drawing at eye level.

- Do whatever relaxation procedures you find useful.

- Concentrate on resting your gaze on the image. Breathe naturally.

- Let your attention explore the edges without losing attention or letting the mind wander. Allow approximately 10 minutes.

This practice can also be used with alternative objects for meditation. Observe the difference when there is already an attachment to the object used as opposed to a more randomly selected one. At the end of the session accept whatever experience has arisen as a mere thought. Relax and let go.

MEDITATION ON AN INTERNAL OBJECT

- Continue this practice with the eyes closed. Re-create or bring to mind the square image. There may be some image distortions

REST IN
THIS SPACE

which are purely physiological due to the retention of the image on the retina; but do not let this distract you.

- Bring to mind the phrase 'The Great Square Has No Corners' and continue to visualize the square.

- Explore the limits of the square and gradually expand your awareness to the furthest limits and see what happens. If your attention wanders or if you are not satisfied with the result (whatever it may be), bring the mind back to the square and start again. Allow approximately 10 minutes.

SOME POSSIBLE REVIEWS

If the square image was enlarged to the greatest possible extent it may eventually lose its corners and become a circle. This is one way of viewing this mysterious paradigm.

- Try this meditation once more, placing yourself at the centre of a cube. Expand the six square sides outwards and watch what happens. In three dimensions, the cube becomes a sphere. This, too, can be expanded in all directions as far as your mind is able to conceive. Fully engage yourself in feeling this experience.
- Rest in this space.

This resting of the mind into spaciousness, without grasping at it or rejecting it, enables the meditator to achieve a sense of 'timelessness' in a fourth dimension (time).

MORE POSSIBLE REVIEWS

The square (also the cruciform) is an archetype denoting the Earth. The perfect square only exists as a concept. It does not appear in nature. The closest is the rhomboid shapes of inert, crystalline structures. It could be said that the square represents the conceptual or finite vision and, when expanded to the infinite, becomes the circle. This could be the inner meaning of the medieval alchemist's preoccupation with the 'squaring of the circle'. So, in summary, the square Earth is transcended by the circle of heaven and the infinite contains the finite. The paradox is that within our finite body form we are able, with the help of the mind, to experience the infinite spaciousness of expanded consciousness.

**Note:** In the meditation each experience of a limitation should be accepted and released as, 'just a thought'. This then becomes an on-going practice and your limitations are no longer obstacles but merely the parameters of your mind.

**A few useful notes:** Once you set a format up, such as the previous meditation, remember that you chose to do it and that it is helpful for you to recognize your commitment.

For example, these following ideas may have been part of your meditational experience:

- A feeling of joy or bliss, followed by:
  *'I've got it, I've got it!'*

- A feeling of fear, followed by:
  *'I've lost it, I've lost it!'*

- A feeling of envy, followed by:
  *'He/she has got it, and I haven't!'*

- A feeling of boredom, followed by:
  *'I don't care anyway!'*

- A feeling of doubt, followed by:
  *'I don't know if I'm doing this right!'*

Emptiness
in form

therefore distractions. Any attachment to, or rejection of them is limiting you. So, find it, recognize it, accept it. This is your 'edge' or limi-

tation. Without the flight or fight reaction, allow yourself to experience this boundary and relax the mind in order to expand it. You can then continue the practice without losing concentration or having to return to the beginning of the technique. In this way, you can enable yourself to handle what could have been an obstacle to your meditation and transform it into part of your practice.

THINGS TO DO
Recognize your insights and:

- enjoy them

- record/write them down, satisfy your need to express. Recognize also that even these creative pursuits are still distractions from the actual practice of meditation. So …

DO IT AGAIN!

Maybe you recognize one or more of these? The list is endless. Maybe you had a unique thought of your own. However, realize that what they are is not important individually. Just realize that they are simply thoughts and

Form in
emptiness

It is essential that one learns to take a state of consciousness achieved through a sitting meditation out into the world. It will remind you that a meditative state is not a rare and exotic flower which only blooms in the hothouse of esoteric meditational practice. Ideally, the meditative state should be part of your everyday life. Even when performing the most mundane tasks, you should endeavour to bring a quality of meditation to them. The famous Chinese and Japanese tea ceremonies are important rituals as well as forms of spiritual meditation. They are ways of bringing full awareness to a simple, everyday task that we all perform, a lesson in extracting enjoyment from anything and everything and living fully in the moment.

One of the best places to start is your first walk outside of the meditational environment. Following your practice, and while still in a mood of concentrated awareness, go for a walk. Bring to bear all the aspects which you have just been practising. Walk purposefully and maintain a quiet, alert mind. Concentrate the mind without tension.

Da Liu, author of T'ai Chi Ch'uan and Meditation, makes the suggestion: 'Walk with the body erect, the shoulders relaxed, and the elbow and knee joints loose … Direct the bulk of your weight below the navel. The foot touching the ground should bear the brunt of your weight while the other foot remains light and weightless.'

In order to allow the toes and feet to move naturally, bare feet or soft, comfortable shoes such as Tai Chi slippers are ideal. The action of placing the whole of the foot (sole, heel and toes) with awareness, acts in the same way as reflexology, increasing the ordinary stimulating effect on the meridians (energy points) as well as veins, glands, nerves, etc.

Notice the action of lifting one foot and placing it in front of you. Be aware of the shift in the body's weight, the contracting and releasing of muscle groups to your feet, of heat and cold, of flexibility and inflexibility. Notice your 'intention' – your intention to make a movement before you make it.

Lift, push, place, lift, push, place, lift, push, place. After practising this technique for the first time young monks often report back to their superiors a whole range of exciting discoveries and insights. They are always told simply to return to their practice. Lift, push, place. It can get even more subtle than that with intention to lift, lift, intention to push, push, intention to place, place.

**Note:** Because of the subtle energies involved in this practice, avoid plastic soles on footwear and walking on concrete. These unnatural materials have the effect of making the flow of energy from earth to body sluggish.

## TAKING AND GIVING: ROOT PRACTICE FOR ERADICATING SUFFERING
*Loving 'oneself' as an act of enlightened self-interest, not as selfishness*

This meditation is from the Tibetan Buddhist tradition and engenders compassion by means of taking the suffering of others and replacing it with the gift of our own happiness. The practice concentrates on the specific nature of the thoughts we have in relation to other people. They can cause us distress of the mind, distress of the emotions and distress of the body. It helps to develop kindness to oneself and others, and as an extra side benefit, a more relaxed and healthy body.

Why should we want to do this? Firstly, to relieve our own pain and suffering often caused by the confusion of not knowing who we really are. It may be helpful to establish that our first aim is to find a way of understanding or transforming our own pain and suffering, from there to find a way of relieving the suffering of others. If we are already dedicated to this goal but have not yet attended to our own needs, it is essential to remember that in order to give love or help to others we have to receive it ourselves, otherwise it is an empty gesture – a bankrupt cannot give generously of money he does not possess. When we truly receive and allow ourselves to be filled with love,

the experience can be so energizing that it spontaneously produces the wish to share that feeling with others. Effortless generosity is the fruit of such a practice.

**Step One:**

### MEDITATION ON GIVING & RECEIVING:
*For understanding and healing relationships between oneself and others*

You've chosen the environment for your practice. You're sitting in a comfortable posture of your choice. You choose your motivation, e.g. you wish to relieve your own suffering.

Now choose an ideal of unconditional, pure, compassionate love. If you belong to a specific religion and however you perceive God, use elements of this image as your model and guide, e.g. the forgiveness of Christ's love, the mother energy of the Virgin Mary, Tara, Shakti, Wakan Tanka (The Great Mystery) of the Native American tradition, or concentrate on the benefits of universal energy, the Mysterious Tao, or remember with gratitude how we are provided with support from our Universe, i.e. food, clothing, shelter, friends, relatives etc. If these fail to inspire, bring to mind the attributes of a living or historical role-model, e.g. the benevolence of Mother Teresa, Florence Nightingale, Gandhi, H.H. the Dalai Lama, or other religious or spiritual leaders.

As an alternative, consider more local or community-based personalities. Closer still, what about your grandparents, a favourite uncle or aunt or loving or inspirational friends. If that loving connection does not lie with an individual but with an environmental situation (a beach or forest, etc.) then imagine yourself sitting          in that nourishing and inspirational setting.

Another suggestion is to look for a time in our lives when we felt loved and cherished by someone near to us and recognize that the capacity for receiving that love is still within.

### MEDITATION PRACTICE:
*for purifying the emotions (obstacles to meditation)*

Imagine the presence of the loving energy. On the in-breath, visualize or feel this energy centring into your heart. This can be in whatever form you feel comfortable, i.e. golden, white or rainbow light, or simply the feeling of warmth and compassion for oneself.

Allow it to mix with any physical pain or mental or emotional negativity which you long to cast off. Discharge this in the form of toxic smoke on the out-breath. If you find this difficult to visualize, then concentrate on the feeling of relief or release.

If you feel that you cannot easily visualize, imagine biting into a lemon and see if this stimulates an increase of saliva flow. Alternatively you could imagine the sound of fingernails screeching down a blackboard!

Continue in this way, receiving love and releasing any negativity, doubts or fears until such a time as there appears to be little or no difference between the in-breath and the out-breath. It is not necessary to dwell on the physical mechanics of breathing as, taken to extremes, this could lead to hyperventilation. Conversely, it is quite common to find oneself spontaneously releasing mental, emotional or physical tension in the form of a deep sigh or involuntary body movements. As always, allow what is natural to occur without judgement or restriction. This, in itself, is a way of ensuring perfect equilibrium.

Step One can constitute a complete practice in its own right, for the inability to receive love is a common imbalance in today's society. This may therefore be a helpful and simple way of practising healing for ourselves. How often have we been moved by the news of some distant disaster and felt ourselves powerless to help, other than possibly on a financial level, thereby doing little to alleviate our own distress. An extension of this technique could be a helpful and simple way of sending healing energy to people we are concerned about, either on a personal level or in a wider context.

The following simple meditation can be an alternative or addition to Tong-Len at this stage.

MEDITATION ON KINDNESS
(METTA BHAVANA):

As long as you can breathe, then you can do this practice. It doesn't involve elaborate preparation or complex mental gymnastics!

Breathing in:    *Being energized.*
Breathing out:   *Wishing others well.*

**Meditation for Children**
*Breathe Sunshine in,*
*Breathe Clouds out.*

**Step Two:** TONG-LEN MEDITATION:
*(for understanding and healing relationships between ourselves and others)*
It can be observed in our day-to-day life that we have basic ways of relating to people, objects and circumstances which we could define as principle forms of reaction. We judge objects and people to be either 'good' or 'bad' in relation to ourselves. That which we deem unimportant we view with indifference. By using this practice it is possible to see the 'relative' nature of this view and how it could be the root cause of all our suffering. For instance, we have all had the experience of being deeply attracted to an individual, even falling in love and, at some later date, disliking or hating them with equal intensity. The very qualities we initially found attractive are often the source of subsequent irritation. So let us examine the basic wishes of all living beings. We wish to be happy and free from suffering. We also wish to be loved unconditionally, free from judgement and limitation. In other words, to be accepted as we are. This meditational practice enables us to recognize this need in ourselves (Step One), and others (Step Two). This can transform many negative emotions and prejudices based on race, class, money, status etc., when we recognize our basic similarities instead of our differences. An excellent form of inter-cultural healing.

THE PRACTICE:
**Choose three people who represent the following qualities:**
a)   **Someone you love**
b)   **Someone to whom you are indifferent**
c)   **Someone you dislike**

Visualize, or bring to mind, the person you have chosen and recognize that they are no different from yourself. You both need love and freedom from suffering. Imagine that their suffering and pain has taken the form of a toxic or smoky cloud, surrounding them and obscuring your view. As you view them with sympathy and compassion you form the wish to take their pain from them and replace it with some of your own happiness.
**Technique:** On the in-breath, breathe this dark energy into your own heart, mix it and transform it into pure energy and on the out-breath return it as

loving compassion. Continue with this practice until they appear smiling and happy. This is a gift from you to the person you love without conditions or desire for any reward other than their good health and well-being. This purifies possessive or selfish love. This is compassion!

## b) Someone to whom you are indifferent

Select a person unknown to you personally (e.g. someone you may have seen passing in the street or on the TV news). This person should be someone who has neither harmed nor pleased you. Follow the same procedures as outlined in the previous technique. They are no different from yourself or the person you love. This will be your unexpected gift to them.

## c) Someone you dislike

Initially, select a person whom you 'dislike' rather than hate, in order to build the practice up in easy steps. (This is really practising compassion on yourself!) A person you dislike is a person you have judged to be unacceptable in your world and you are attempting to push them away or deny their existence. By selecting them as a subject for your practice you are allowing yourself to suspend judgement and respect their right to be who they are. In other words, you like to be unconditionally accepted and you are prepared to extend this kindness to them.

'Re-spect' can be regarded as having a chance to look again. Repeat the technique of taking their unhappiness and giving them your happiness in return.

You may well think this is the most difficult part of the practice. However, compare this with the pain of letting go of someone you love. There are usually only a very few people we passionately love or hate because the emotions take up so much energy. In comparison, how many other countless billions are there that we have not even thought about and to whose suffering we are indifferent: we will never be short of people who could benefit from our help in this area. This can be a way of transmuting or transforming our 'passion' into 'compassion' and become more loving and peaceful as a result of our understanding and commitment to change.

Our understanding is that we are no different from others. What we wish to receive as unconditional love, we practise giving. What we wish to give, we practise receiving. There is no difference. Balancing the two brings peace and equanimity. As our indifference to suffering diminishes, our ability to grow with love and awareness increases.

This practice enables us to clear up the emotional pollution that clouds our relationships bringing clarity and peace of mind which reduces mental and physical tension and serves to heal the conflict within ourselves. In the

early stages we are removing the emotions we project onto others, creating a space for something positive to happen. We are acknowledging that we are creating our own suffering in the way that we relate to other beings and that we have the capacity to change. We then have the choice between being overwhelmed by our emotions or transmuting them into a form of healing, connecting energy.

One way of coping with strong or unpleasant emotions is to discharge them. With Tong-Len, however, we can transform them from exhausting, destructive energy, to something we can actually utilize. Taking an alternative view of human or animal waste products, a farmer or gardener can transform something (viewed as 'bad') into compost (viewed as 'good'). In the East this process is regarded as using the transformative power of the emotions as fuel for enlightenment. In other words, there is no longer any need to fear the strength of our 'negative' emotions. They can be turned on their head to produce even greater insights.

**Step Three:** TONG-LEN MEDITATION
*Having compassion on oneself*
In order to prevent any unconscious retention of negative energies, return to Step One where, once again, you have the opportunity to receive unconditional love from your original source. This is a form of protection. As

Shantideva says:

*'Whoever wishes to quickly afford protection to both himself and others should practise that holy secret: the exchanging of self for others'*

The meditation can be concluded by offering up the results or 'merit' of the practice to the benefit of all (sentient) beings. This unselfish dedication emphasizes our understanding that there is no difference between ourselves and others. Eventually, you may even be able to thank those with whom you were once angry for providing the incentive for you to initiate your own healing process.

Many stories abound in Tibet, of people with incurable diseases, e.g. leprosy, who took up this practice as a preparation for death. To their own astonishment and that of family and friends, they returned home after diligent practice, cured of their physical infirmity.

### ATTACHMENT, AVERSION AND BOREDOM

There are many things which can distract attention during meditation. Take noise, for example. Even after a place has been prepared where you would expect minimum distraction you may notice a noise creeping into your consciousness. Your reaction to it is based on how you 'judge' it. If you decide that it is 'unpleasant', then the noise will cause you suffering. Your negative emotions result from not accepting it as as mere sound, neither good nor bad. Suspend judgement, recognize your reaction as one of many other thoughts, let it go, and bring your mind home to the task in hand.

Conversely, an 'attractive' sound is another kind of noise, such as an unexpected burst of birdsong. Through our conditioning, we would tend to accept this as an attractive background addition to our meditational practice with its accompanying 'rewards' and blissful state. Recognize your perception of this as 'just a thought' and a manifestation of our habitual addiction to 'good feelings'. This is a pleasant distraction but a distraction nonetheless. It is an intrinsic need within ourselves to feel we must ascribe different qualities to what simply 'is' or exists in its own right. If we become attached to the birdsong, we could suffer a sense of loss when it eventually ceases. So, let go of this thought, return to the practice and ...

### DO IT AGAIN!

### BOREDOM AND ENNUI (INDIFFERENCE)

This is a defence mechanism that comes into play when we get close to the truth as a result of meditation: a cessation of grasping or attachment to 'good thoughts' and a pushing away or aversion to 'bad thoughts'. This sometimes results in a mixture of apathy, fear and disenchantment, a kind of limbo or no-man's land. This state is not so much one of equanimity or equilibrium but of suspended animation. The energetic dynamic between the polarities has been arrested, not balanced.

### BLISS STATE, FEAR STATE

These are strong emotions generally thought of as respectively 'positive' and 'negative'. To the meditator there is no difference between these and feelings of boredom. They are equal distractions within any form of discipline. These states can be transmuted in a practice such as Tong-Len (see page 180). However, in 'awareness meditation' it is sufficient to know that it becomes an obstacle if you wrestle with them, either to embrace them or to push them away. The powerful waves of bliss can be overwhelmingly attractive. A great Catholic mystic warned those who would indulge in this state that they risked becoming like 'bees caught in their own honey'.

As meditation deepens, so does the intensity of our experience of these

emotional states. Far from being an indication that we are poor at meditation, this can indicate how close we are to recognizing a truer state of mind. When these obstacles appear, and we are prepared to simply continue with the practice, they can bring to light our hidden resources and deepen our commitment. These so-called 'bad experiences' are merely the uncovering of yet another layer of the mind. Use them as a basis for the next stage of practice or, alternatively, continue to observe the arising emotions, recognizing them as just intangible, illusory thoughts and let them go. In other words, return to your practice and
DO IT AGAIN!

### DOUBTS & RESERVATIONS

The initial feelings of awareness to come to the surface, through the focus of one-pointed meditation or concentration, will make you realize just how mentally undisciplined you are. The mind at this stage has been variously described as 'monkey mind' or 'unbroken horse' and compared to a 'rudderless ship' adrift on a sea of confusion. Meditational practices are aimed at 'taming the wild mind-flow'. Commitment to training and tuning the mind is of tantamount importance, just as an athlete or dancer trains the body.

Although this may seem daunting, all that is necessary at first is to practise for a short time each day. Devote as

much time as you can manage, and don't try to compete with yourself (the antithesis of meditation). After a while, your practice will become habitual, but a useful habit rather than an unhelpful one. A classic image is that of a pot which fills, little by little, a drop at a time, until it is full.

If at this time you feel that you still don't know enough, perhaps this story will inspire you. The fame of a legendary meditation master reached the ears of a learned professor. He arranged a meeting with the Master and, while waiting for him to serve the traditional tea, told him of his position at the University and his years of concentrated study. The Master smiled amiably while pouring the tea into the professor's cup. As the professor continued to regale him with his accomplishments, the Master continued to pour tea into an already full cup. The professor pointed this out with astonishment. The Master looked at him and said: 'You are like this cup, full to overflowing. Until you empty yourself I am unable to give you anything.'

So, if you are a beginner, congratulations, you have an empty cup. This state of consciousness is known as 'Zen Mind, Beginner's Mind' and indicates the freshness and openness of a humble mind.

BENEFITS OF MEDITATION
The physical body takes a time to reach a peak of condition and strength so, in

all probability, it will take time to experience the benefits of regular meditation. If you expect a golden chariot to sweep you off to the heavens and rescue you from yourself, you may be disappointed! Perhaps, with every new insight, you hope to be greeted with a roar of approval from the hosts of cosmic beings about you. It might happen, but then again it may not. The expectation that enlightenment will suddenly occur in a blaze of glory is a tricky belief and may hinder progress. Our understanding often comes as a painful realization of our own ignorance. All too often, the very practices designed to liberate us can chain us to a misguided ideal which we can't live up to. The following Zen *koan* is a paradoxical riddle about the nature of existence or eternal truth. *Koans* are given by spiritual masters to educate their students to free themselves from their mental preconceptions.

*'What is the sound of one hand clapping?'*
This is a source of contemplation rather than an intellectual conundrum. However, this did not prevent the publication of a book offering Westerners 100 *koans* and their answers! The *koans* are designed to shock the conditioned mind out of old dualistic forms of thinking by presenting it with seemingly unsolvable questions. The benefits lie in the process of realization, not in the 'answer'. After

realization, the Zen Master simply gives the student another appropriate *koan*. Similarly, in our meditational practice, realizations and insights will arise. Try to avoid the need to share your discoveries with all and sundry: let them go and settle back into your regular meditational practice.

St. John of the Cross observed: 'He who interrupts the course of his spiritual exercises and prayer is like a man who allows a bird to escape from his hand: he can hardly catch it again.'

To obtain the greatest benefit from regular practice, realize that ten minutes of quality, committed meditation is better than an hour of dutiful or unfocused practice. Choose a time and duration to which you can commit yourself without feeling you are neglecting other areas of your life. Make it a daily requirement, a good habit such as brushing your teeth. When you start to feel the benefits you will not begrudge your commitment.

*'There's only one failure in meditation – the failure to meditate.'*

WAKING UP THE MIND
In the early morning, after a good night's sleep, get up immediately. Experience shows that 'dozing' for that extra hour is often counterproductive. Your consciousness slides confusedly between the two distinct states of waking and dreaming. A practice called 'Dream Yoga' could enable you

to take your awareness with you into sleep time, utilizing the lucid state in order to extend your spiritual practices. This is an advanced practice for adepts but, for most of us, it is sufficient to 'wake up' in our 'daytime' dream and progress from there.

One of the side benefits of regular meditation is to decrease the amount of sleep required. This makes, 'I'd like to meditate but I haven't got time' rather an invalid excuse. Meditation can provide you with the extra time you need!

Meditation is all about BEING IN THE HERE AND NOW, not in the future or past, not in a trance, not in the middle of some romantic 'space opera' loading ourselves with distractions rather than bravely confronting the all-powerful NOW. You may have heard or used the phrase:'The lights are on, but there is nobody at home'. Meditation is a way of coming home.

TAKING THE BENEFITS INTO YOUR DAILY LIFE
Once you have a basic understanding of the simple principles involved, you will be eager to grasp any opportunity of filling the natural spaces which appear in any full and busy day. Just recognize these 'gaps' which occur between your everyday chores and relax into them. This can include such simple things as walking in a park, making tea, sitting quietly with awareness, etc. St. Thérèse de Lisieux gave

absolute and minute attention to everyday tasks, confirming the importance of every second in what she called her 'little way'.

Meditation can intensify negative traits as well as bringing welcome benefits. This can occur after concentrated practice when you relax back into an everyday situation. Try to take your awareness with you and be alert to subtle or dramatic changes in lifestyle, attitudes and experiences. The purification of 'unhealthy' states of mind may produce a temporary effect similar to the 'healing crisis' experienced during a physical detoxification process.

As you may well expect to read this once again (with increased compassion) return to your practice and …

DO IT AGAIN!

Consistent practice in such arts as single-pointedness, or any exercise in concentration, enables you to learn to do one thing at a time. In meditation we reduce the tendency for the mind to skip about between this and that. If your attention is not also 'mindful' of what you are doing there will be a split focus and the mind's dualistic nature will still be apparent. While engaged in everyday tasks, you should be aware that whatever you are doing you can also experience it more directly by cultivating an attitude of mindfulness. When doing something, just do it. As a result, the simplicity of the famous Zen saying: 'When I eat, I eat. When I sleep, I sleep', becomes less obscure

and more about our ordinary human life.

Following this observation, we can say: 'When I meditate, I meditate'. We simply do it, paradoxically, without expectations. The following Zen aphorisms illustrate the process of enlightenment along this journey into supreme consciousness.

*'Before enlightenment*
*gathering twigs*
*carrying water.*
*After enlightenment*
*gathering twigs*
*carrying water'*

This *koan* illustrates the point that meditation does not take you to some 'other-worldly' place. You stay truly within yourself. You may still carry on the daily tasks and routines of your current everyday life but you will bring a new awareness to them so that they become subtly different. Your consciousness will grow in awareness and the most mundane of acts will take on a new significance.

*'To a beginner on the Path*
*A tree is a tree,*
*a mountain is a mountain.*
*To one who is treading the path,*
*a tree is no longer a tree,*
*a mountain no longer a mountain!*
*To one who has realized the Path*
*A tree is once more a tree,*
*a mountain once more a mountain'*

By cultivating an open view you can expect the unexpected: without restrictions you can achieve the true benefits of meditation which are limitless. No beginning, no end. In our ignorance we strayed onto the Path for in the presence of Pure Natural Mind there is no Path, no Journey …

WE ARE ALREADY HOME!

## DO I NEED A MEDITATION TEACHER?

The answer is, 'almost certainly', at least at some stage. I'm sure there must be cases where devotees have learnt all there is to know from a book, but it's not just about learning techniques. The profound psychological changes brought about by such powerful techniques can be literally life-changing and a whole host of questions are likely to arise: Am I doing the practice correctly? What do I do if I find myself suddenly swamped by anger/fear/jealousy etc? As constantly reiterated, the answer simply lies in returning to the practice and doing it again. However, religious/spiritual systems are a treasure-house of practical knowledge about such matters and are inhabited by people just like you who are practising and in many cases having experiences which parallel your own. To ignore all that potential guidance would be unwise.

The Yogic tradition of India has a term, Setsang, which broadly translated means 'fellowship with truth' (also implying the search for truth). In the early stages of meditation you are like a young sapling, subject to harsh winds, blown in many directions. Yet if you choose to associate with like-minded people who aspire to useful meditation (other saplings) you are together less susceptible to damage, especially in those vulnerable early stages of experience.

Most traditions of religion and belief either accept or would insist upon practice in conjunction with teachers and other students as one of the most important prerequisites of the quest for spiritual growth. This is certainly true of the major religions: Christians and Jews congregate to pray, contemplate and meditate, Muslims in a mosque, Hindus in temples and Buddhists have the concept of Sangha, the Vajrayana path, for instance, insisting that the presence of a teacher is essential.

What to Look For in a Teacher
If you decide to look for a teacher, look first to personal recommendation. If you don't know anyone who practises meditation, go to your public library and look for lists of groups and organizations.

You would do well to consider the following points when evaluating a potential teacher or group:

- Is the teacher, method or group in sympathy with your deepest goals and general disposition? Be wary of any that seek to deny your highest aspirations.

- Be wary of any person or group demanding large sums of money up front before being prepared to reveal any of their precious teachings.

- Does the teacher personally embody the benefits claimed to result from their method? Are they compassionate, calm, understanding and tolerant?

- Is the teacher committed to their method/path and do they communicate clearly?

- Is the teacher more concerned about their goals than yours?

- Does the teacher spontaneously respond to your needs and do they inspire and instill confidence in your ability to stand on your own two feet?

- A teacher should be a true 'spiritual friend' who will serve to mirror your 'good' and 'bad' qualities. When you get to the point where you genuinely wish to follow a spiritual path, you must be willing to accept both.

- Remember, the beauty and wisdom you see in any teacher is but a reflection of those qualities which exist in yourself.

In any teacher-student relationship, it is difficult to follow the true spiritual approach and not fall into the trap of habitual over-expectation. In the beginning, you should rely on your natural instincts and not dwell too deeply on the whys and wherefores of your choice – follow your feelings.

As meditation deepens, emotions, cravings, compulsions and fears begin to lose their energy and power over us. In this new climate of openness choice is now a possibility. So, why not liberate yourself from addictive habits and negative behaviour by recognizing them for what they are and choosing not to be controlled by them. We are empowered with the ability to live more positively, with free will, as God and our true natures intended.

Buddha said: 'All that we are is a result of what we have thought.' By changing our *modus operandi* (way of operating), we change our habit of conditioned thinking and thereby change ourselves.

### RELATIVE BELIEF
*Meditation is the Activity of 'Doing' and the Ultimate View is the Activity of 'Being'*

It must be admitted that any opinions or viewpoints expressed in this book are relative and subject to amendment. None of them are solid truths, set in stone. We have to be more open and flexible than that. Hopefully, some of the ideas will give you a taste for meditation and a different perspective on the subject of human existence.

What we offer here is our highest truth as we see it. By embracing and accepting it we have exposed ourselves to the possibility of developing a more expanded view, and you must learn to do the same. If we pretend to be the guardians of knowledge we do not in fact possess, we only serve to arrest our own spiritual growth and this is not a useful activity. All we can work with is our truth as we perceive it. We take part in the activity and engage in the business of it. Everything else is a mere distraction.

### ULTIMATE VIEW
During meditation, when confusion arises, recognize its 'relative' nature, relax and allow it to resolve into the 'Absolute'. Rediscover and rest in your sky-like nature.

'Rest in natural great peace
This exhausted mind
Beaten helplessly by karma*
And neurotic thought
Like the relentless fury of pounding waves
in the infinite ocean of Samsara**

\* *karma* – the law of cause and effect
\*\* *Samsara* – the world of suffering and delusion

Text by Nyoshul Khen Rinpoche from *Songs of Experience*, Rigpa, London, 1989.

### A SIMPLE TRUTH
You already know all you need to know about meditation. It is so simple that you will find it difficult to grasp this fundamental idea – to be what you already are! This book will help you complicate things and either satisfy your need to be elaborate or make you so tired of the complexities that you'll be willing to drop your resistance to relaxing into your natural state of being.

So, stop right here. Look directly into your mind and ...

### BE HERE IN THE NOW